LIVING A GODLY LIFE

DISCOVER PERSONAL GROWTH & THE WAY TO A SUCCESSFUL LIFE

APRIL 2013

To MY FRIENDS,
STEVE & MARTHA MORGAN,

THANK YOU FOR YOUR EXAMPLE
OF WHAT IT MEANS TO LIVE A
GODLY LIFE!
YOU BRING 2 TIMOTHY 2:2
TO LIFE!
AT YOUR SERVICE,

LIVING A GODLY LIFE

DISCOVER PERSONAL GROWTH &
THE WAY TO A SUCCESSFUL LIFE

~ †††† ~

HAL MOROZ

NEW YORK   ATLANTA   WASHINGTON   MEXICO CITY   BEIJING

Living a Godly Life:
Discover Personal Growth & The Way to a Successful Life
Hal Moroz

Copyright © 2013 by Harold Ronald Moroz

First Edition

Unless otherwise noted, Scripture quotations are from
The King James Version of the Bible.

Scripture taken from the New King James Version®.
Copyright © 1982 by Thomas Nelson, Inc.
Used by permission.
All rights reserved.

The text of the New King James Version® (NKJV®) may be quoted or reprinted without prior written permission with the following qualifications: (1) up to and including 1,000 verses may be quoted in printed form so long as the verses quoted amount to less than 50% of a complete book of the Bible and make up less than 50% of the total work in which they are quoted; (2) all NKJV quotations must conform accurately to the NKJV text.

For quotation requests not covered by the above guidelines, write to
Thomas Nelson, Inc., Attention: Bible Rights and Permissions,
P.O. Box 141000, Nashville, TN 37214-1000.

Scripture taken from the NEW AMERICAN STANDARD BIBLE®,
Copyright © 1960,1962,1963,1968,1971,1972,1973,1975,1977,1995
by The Lockman Foundation.
Used by Permission.

The opinions expressed in this book are solely the opinions of the author and do not necessarily reflect the opinions of any individual, groups, organizations or business entities mentioned herein.
The quotes, selected writings, and articles contained in this book are reprinted with permission or are permissible for use under existing law.

Printed in the United States of America

Living a Godly Life:
Discover Personal Growth & The Way to a Successful Life

"But Jesus beheld them, and said unto them, With men this is impossible;
but with God all things are possible."
~~~ Matthew 19:26

Living a Godly Life:
Discover Personal Growth & The Way to a Successful Life
Hal Moroz

Contents

Introduction
Behold the Kingdom of God

~ ~ ~ ~ ~

"Verily I say unto you,
Whosoever shall not receive the kingdom of God as a little child
shall in no wise enter therein."
~~~ Mark 10:15

~ ~ ~ ~ ~

In this age of cynicism, where we are taught to question all things, including authority, it is a difficult thing to walk in optimism, faith and hope. From the moment we leave the innocence of childhood, we are exposed to a myriad of shattering realities. The world tells us many things: People lie. They deceive. They make bold pronouncements that shake our faith. They betray and they forsake one another for selfish reasons, personal gain and ambition. And, among other things, love fails.

But there is an alternative. A way to live life optimistically, dwelling on good things, and with the virtues of faith, hope and love at the forefront. This is living life more abundantly. This is living a godly life. And that is what this book is all about. It is a guide that points the way to Truth, and in that Truth, an anchor that grounds us to an immovable foundation.

Is this too good to be true? No! Not if you have faith, and hope, and most of all, love. But it all starts with a leap of faith, like that of a little child. A willingness to accept help in this difficult journey we call Life. Proverbs 8:33 states, *"Hear instruction, and be wise, and refuse it not."* This is key! And Proverbs 9:9 builds on this proposition by stating, *"Give instruction to a wise man, and he will* be yet wiser: teach a just man, and he will increase in learning." So boldly accept godly instruction! Be wise! And learn!

Accept truth, even when the world tells you it may not be reasonable. Do not be afraid or embarrassed. Be of great joy. And embrace the proposition that there is more to life than the brief shining moment we spend on earth.

In Isaiah 41:10, we read:

> [10] Do not fear, for I am with you; Do not anxiously look about you, for I am your God. I will strengthen you, surely I will help you, Surely I will uphold you with My righteous right hand. [NASB]

So there is no mistake, and no sense of being deceived, let me make this perfectly clear: This is a book about the love of God. And how you can benefit from that unconditional love and the promises He makes to you. The Bible is replete with admonitions from God for you and me to *fear not*[1] and to be *anxious*[2] *for nothing*. He says these words for a reason. And as 2 Timothy 1:7 reminds us, *"For God hath not given us the spirit of fear; but of power, and of love, and of a sound mind."* Know that whatever problems, difficulties or challenges you face, no matter how dire they may seem, God can and will help you. Victory is within your grasp, and it is not by chance you are reading these very words. God has a purpose and a plan for you! My friends, I speak from personal experience. And all you have to do is believe!

---

[1] Genesis 15:1, 21:17, 26:24, 35:17, 43:23, 46:3, 50:21; Exodus 14:13, 20:20; Numbers 1:34; Deuteronomy 1:21, 3:2, 3:22, 20:3, 31:6, 31:8; Joshua 8:1, 10:25; Judges 4:18, 6:10, 6:23; Ruth 3:11; 1 Samuel 12:20, 22:23, 23:17; 2 Samuel 9:7, 13:28; 1 Kings 17:13; 2 Kings 6:16, 17:35, 17:37, 17:38, 25:24; 1 Chronicles 28:20; 2 Chronicles 20:17; Job 11:15; Psalm 27:3, 56:4, 118:6; Proverbs 3:25; Isaiah 7:4, 8:12, 35:4, 41:10, 41:13, 41:14, 43:1, 43:5, 44:2, 44:8, 51:7, 54:4, 54:14; Jeremiah 40:9, 46:27, 46:28; Lamentations 3:57; Ezekiel 3:9; Daniel 10:12, 10:19; Joel 2:21; Zephaniah 3:16; Haggai 2:5; Zechariah 8:13, 8:15; Matthew 1:20, 10:26, 10:28, 10:31, 28:5; Luke 1:13, 1:30, 2:10, 5:10, 8:50, 12:7, 12:32; John 12:15; Acts 27:24; 2 Timothy 1:7; Hebrews 13:6; 1 John 4:18; Revelation 1:17.
[2] Isaiah 41:10; Jeremiah 17:8; Philippians 4:6.

But no matter where you are in life, this book has something for you! You may be searching for personal growth or success, or both. You may already be successful. You may be part of what the world calls the *"underprivileged"* or the *"middle class"* or the *"top 1%."* You may be unemployed, working, a student, retired, or a homemaker. You may be a sinner or saved, a sales person on the floor of a local department store or a member of the clergy. It does not matter. You will be better off for having read this book, because it holds within these pages a timeless truth. I promise that if you read this book and apply the principles contained herein, you will experience a changed life!

As an attorney and counselor at law, former law school professor and judge, I have spent a significant amount of my life studying, teaching, and applying the Law. In a very meaningful way, this book is about the Law, but it is also about Grace. The former was handed down through Moses in the Ten Commandments,[3] which established the very foundation of our current civil and criminal laws. *"Thou shalt not kill."*[4] *"Thou shalt not commit adultery."*[5] *"Thou shalt not steal."*[6] *"Thou shalt not bear false witness against thy neighbor."*[7] These are each part of the Ten Commandments, and they are obvious statutes we can readily find in the legal codes of our modern civilization. But in many ways, they are statutes that condemn, being punishable under the Law when violated. I dare say you could not find a human being alive on our planet that has not been in violation of at least one of these commandments under the law during his or her lifetime.

However, Grace is another matter. It is a gift from God.[8] And Grace is a state separate and above the Law. Grace allows us

---

[3] Exodus 34:28.
[4] Exodus 20:13.
[5] Exodus 20:14.
[6] Exodus 20:15.
[7] Exodus 20:16.
[8] Romans 5:15.

to live godly lives, whereas only perfect adherence to the Law allows us to live a life free of prosecution. Perfection is an exceedingly high standard, and any transgression or sin under the law is punishable. In fact, perfection is too high a standard for man to achieve without God, as we suffer from a sin nature.[9] In His Word, God states:

> [23] For all have sinned, and come short of the glory of God;
>
> [24] Being justified freely by his grace through the redemption that is in Christ Jesus:
>
> [25] Whom God hath set forth to be a propitiation through faith in his blood, to declare his righteousness for the remission of sins that are past, through the forbearance of God;
>
> [26] To declare, I say, at this time his righteousness: that he might be just, and the justifier of him which believeth in Jesus. [Romans 3:23-26]

In effect, there are two states of being: Under the Law or under Grace. Living under the Law is a state of being that condemns you once you sin,[10] but living under Grace removes the sin that would separate us from God.[11] *"For sin shall not have dominion over you,"* states Roman 6:14, *"for ye are not under the law, but under grace."* And Galatians 2:21 states, *"for if righteousness come by the law, then Christ is dead in vain."* The Lord Jesus Christ did not die in vain! *"For the law was given by Moses,"* John 1:17 enlightens us, *"but grace and the truth came by Jesus Christ."*

---

[9] Romans 3:23.
[10] Ezekiel 18:4.
[11] Romans 6:23.

Finally, it is important to note that Grace does not relieve us from our duty to obey the Law, that being, the Commandments of God and the laws of governments, as long as the latter do not conflict with the Word of God. In John 14:15, Jesus says, *"If ye love me, keep my commandments."* This is not an option, it is a command. We are to obey His commandments. These include the original Ten and all others brought forth in Holy Scripture through guidance from the Holy Spirit. And Jesus further commanded our respect and obedience for man-made law in Matthew 22:21, when He said, *"Render therefore unto Caesar the things which are Caesar's; and unto God the things that are God's."*[12]

While it may seem strange to some to have an attorney write a book on godly living, think about it in context of the Holy Bible. The apostle Paul was originally a strict advocate of the Law. He even stood by in support of those that stoned to death Stephen, the first Christian martyr.[13] Paul was an enemy of the fledgling Christian church, but it was God's plan for his life that he should be a powerful evangelist of the Gospel of Jesus Christ. And he was. Paul answered God's call to preach the Word of God, and his impact is still felt today.

Not that I am in any way putting myself in Paul's league, I am not. I consider myself a mere babe in the study of God's Word, for it contains within its pages the very sum total of all knowledge and understanding for the benefit of all mankind. In the Holy Bible is the answer to all, and I do mean all, the problems and challenges facing man. It has all the answers you will ever need to be successful and grow and to live a godly life. In Micah 6:8 we read, *"He hath shewed thee, O man, what is good; and what doth the LORD require of thee, but to do justly, and to love mercy, and to walk humbly with thy God?"* I am learning new things every day, and in my walk of faith and understanding, I understand that I have a privilege and a duty to share what I have learned. It is my hope that

---

[12] *See also* Mark 12:17 & Luke 20:25.
[13] Acts 7:58 - 8:1.

you will do this as well.

In this work, my focus is on the fact that we are all lost without God in our lives. And the beauty of it is God accepts us just as we are. He then does a work in our lives. In my life, I find the more I grow in my walk with the Lord, the more I am compelled to share His life-changing Gospel. I learn, and I share. And I find time after time this simple sharing does wonders in the lives of friends and associates who struggle with despair and anxiety. It is something Scripture commands us to do.[14] None of us are called to take this walk of faith alone.

This book is important for several compelling reasons. It is a glimpse of God's unconditional love, and His acceptance of you just as you are! Like Paul, it doesn't matter what you did in your past. *"Therefore if any man be in Christ, he is a new creature,"* writes Paul in 2 Corinthians 5:17, *"old things are passed away; behold, all things are become new."* This is the power of the Gospel of Jesus Christ. It is life-changing!

And this is a book that encourages, provides hope, and gives meaning to life, because it is a commentary on the Gospel. I have heard it said by one friend in the faith that the Gospel is best defined as: *"The Good News of Jesus Christ and His offer of salvation through His death, burial, and resurrection, that we receive through faith."*[15]

It is my prayer that you are reading this book because you are seeking God's hand upon your life. Alternatively, perhaps you are reading this book because someone thought well enough of you to share the essence of this Good News with you. 1 Peter 4:10 tells us, *"As every man hath received the gift, even so minister the same one*

---

[14] Hebrews 10:13; Hebrews 10:25; Romans 14:19; 1 Corinthians 14:26; 2 Corinthians 12:19; Ephesians 4:12; Ephesians 4:16; Ephesians 4:29; 1 Thessalonians 5:11; 1 Timothy 1:4.

[15] Dr. Charles F. Stanley, Senior Pastor, First Baptist Church of Atlanta, 2012.

to another, as good stewards of the manifold grace of God." Now that is living a godly life at its very best!

As I mentioned earlier, I learn and I share. It is my hope that you will do the same. And as I continue to learn, I am persuaded that this book is just a beginning, a work in progress: The first of many on the subject, as I do not intend to stagnate in my walk or my life. I have pledged to learn every day and share the Good News of the Kingdom of God.

I began this Introduction by telling you what the world thinks about many things, including Love. But let me cut to the chase, and conclude this passage on a positive note. After all, that is what this work is all about. Let me tell you what God says about Love:

> [4] Love is patient, love is kind and is not jealous; love does not brag and is not arrogant,
>
> [5] does not act unbecomingly; it does not seek its own, is not provoked, does not take into account a wrong suffered,
>
> [6] does not rejoice in unrighteousness, but rejoices with the truth;
>
> [7] bears all things, believes all things, hopes all things, endures all things. [1 Corinthians 13:4-7, NASB]

Now that we know about Love, let us apply what God shares in 1 John 4:7, *"Beloved, let us love one another: for love is of God; and every one that loveth is born of God, and knoweth God."* Know God! And trust the truth He exclaims in the very next verse of the previous reading in 1 Corinthians, *"Love never fails."*[16] My friends, believe, and *"receive the kingdom of God as a little child."*[17]

---

[16] 1 Corinthians 13:8, NASB.
[17] Mark 10:15.

Behold the Kingdom of God ...

~~~~~~~~~~

*"And the things that thou hast heard of me among many witnesses,
the same commit thou to faithful men, who shall be able to teach others also."*
~~~ 2 Timothy 2:2

Chapter 1
Godly Living

~ ~ ~ ~ ~

"To sum up, all of you be harmonious,
sympathetic, brotherly, kindhearted, and humble in spirit;
Not returning evil for evil or insult for insult, but giving a blessing instead;
For you were called for the very purpose that you might inherit a blessing.
For, The one who desires life, to love and see good days,
Must keep his tongue from evil and do good;
He must seek peace and pursue it.
For the eyes of the Lord are toward the righteous,
And His ears attend to their prayer,
But the face of the Lord is against those who do evil."
~~~ 1 Peter 3:8-12, NASB

~ ~ ~ ~ ~

I am always amazed at the simple and direct instructions contained in Holy Scripture for leading a godly life. Think about the above quote from 1 Peter 3:9, *"Not returning evil for evil or insult for insult, but giving a blessing instead; For you were called for the very purpose that you might inherit a blessing."* This totally diffuses bad feelings or potential arguments among people, not to mention family members or spouses. What an amazing concept that we should be *"a blessing"* to those we might encounter in our lives!

This is the simplicity and the power of the Holy Bible. It has all we need to understand and achieve a godly life, the keys to personal growth, and the path to success. It is God's gift to the human race, and contains the blueprint for successful living, how to help guide the ones we love, and to correct them when they are stumbling, and how to keep them on a successful path. As 2 Timothy 3:16-17 states, *"[16]All scripture is given by inspiration of*

God, and is profitable for doctrine, for reproof, for correction, for instruction in righteousness: [17]That the man of God may be perfect, thoroughly furnished unto all good works."

Godly living is living life at its very best. It is living life with great and sometimes unimaginable success. And Holy Scripture tells us that this success is not for a season, but a lifetime! It is true prosperity! Read and marvel at the words of Psalm 1:

> [1] Blessed is the man that walketh not in the counsel of the ungodly, nor standeth in the way of sinners, nor sitteth in the seat of the scornful.
>
> [2] But his delight is in the law of the LORD; and in his law doth he meditate day and night.
>
> [3] And he shall be like a tree planted by the rivers of water, that bringeth forth his fruit in his season; his leaf also shall not wither; and whatsoever he doeth shall prosper.
>
> [4] The ungodly are not so: but are like the chaff which the wind driveth away.
>
> [5] Therefore the ungodly shall not stand in the judgment, nor sinners in the congregation of the righteous.
>
> [6] For the LORD knoweth the way of the righteous: but the way of the ungodly shall perish.

Psalm 1 is a clear and common sense approach to life. This is godly living! To walk with other good and godly people, to avoid evil and scornful people, to follow the laws of God, to be a blessing to others, and know that godly living is the way to success and prosperity. These are the words and promises of God. Meditate on them and follow them!

With this in mind, let's take a look at the fundamentals of this all important Word of God. Is It Really Important? Who Wrote It? Does It apply to me?

Is the Holy Bible Really Important?

So the real first question we must answer is: *Is the Holy Bible really important?* The answer is: *Absolutely!* This must be distinctly understood, or nothing good can come from this wonderful journey I am about to relate. The Bible is the Word of God. It is His unfolding revelation to mankind. It is the key to immediate, short-term, long-term, and eternal prosperity and success.

In the Holy Bible, we read the following in John 1:1-5:

> [1] In the beginning was the Word, and the Word was with God, and the Word was God.
>
> [2] The same was in the beginning with God.
>
> [3] All things were made by Him; and without Him was not any thing made that was made.
>
> [4] In Him was life; and the life was the light of men.
>
> [5] And the light shineth in darkness; and the darkness comprehended it not.

Through these verses, we find that the Word of God is key to walking in the light of God. Without It, we are walking in darkness.

And John 1:14, goes on to state, *"And the Word was made flesh, and dwelt among us, (and we beheld His glory, the glory as of the only begotten of the Father,) full of grace and truth."* This is Christ Jesus.

And know that speaking the Word of God is important because of its impact, as we shall see throughout this book. It actually changes lives! And you are instrumental in this process when you share the Gospel. Psalm 37:23 tells us, *"The steps of a good man are ordered by the LORD: and he delighteth in his way."* And as we read the Word of God and speak it to others, God tells us in Isaiah 55:11: *"So shall my word be that goeth forth out of my mouth: it shall not return unto me void, but it shall accomplish that which I please, and it shall prosper in the thing whereto I sent it."* Speaking the Word of God is powerful, and always serves God's purpose. So speak it!

Who Wrote the Holy Bible?

The Holy Bible was written by the hands of many godly men, starting with the writing of Genesis by Moses and ending with the Book of Revelation by the apostle John, who were inspired by the Holy Spirit. It was written over the span of 1400 years and covers more than 4000 years of mankind's history.

Sceptics will question how men could have written of events prior to their births *(such as by Moses in Genesis)* and following their deaths *(such as by the prophets and the apostle John in Revelation)*. But the mere fact that men accurately wrote of these events gives us insight into the Bible's true authorship. God revealed those things that we might otherwise not have known. In 2 Peter 1:21, we read: *"For the prophecy came not in old time by the will of man: but holy men of God spake as they were moved by the Holy Ghost."* The author of the Holy Bible is God, with the words penned by prophets and the holy men of old.

Does the Holy Bible Apply to Me?

Knowing that the Holy Bible is both important and an inspired work of God, it merits asking: *Does the Holy Bible apply to me?* The answer is an unequivocal: *Yes!*

If you desire to live a godly life, to grow personally, be successful, be righteous, and be a man or woman after God's own heart, then the Holy Bible is indispensable! As we noted earlier, and as 2 Timothy 3:16-17 states, *"¹⁶All scripture is given by inspiration of God, and is profitable for doctrine, for reproof, for correction, for instruction in righteousness: ¹⁷That the man of God may be perfect, thoroughly furnished unto all good works."* Know with all of your heart, and soul, and mind, it was written for you! You are special to God. Yes, the God who created the universe and made all things is personally interested in you and your future. Here is what God says: *"For I know the plans that I have for you,' declares the Lord, 'plans for welfare and not for calamity to give you a future and a hope."*[18] He gave you and me the Word so that we might have a restored close and personal relationship with Him. He loves you! Believe in Him, and trust Him! His Word applies to you!

But knowing these things and all that you read in this book will matter little if you do not take that leap of faith I spoke about earlier. This is a time of decision-making, that is, making a decision to believe in the power of God to change your life or pursuing other paths. It is the choice we read about in the Book of Joshua. *"Now therefore fear the LORD, and serve him in sincerity and in truth: and put away the gods which your fathers served on the other side of the flood, and in Egypt; and serve ye the LORD,"* we read in Joshua 24:15, and the pivotal decision in the very next verse, *"And if it seem evil unto you to serve the LORD, choose you this day whom ye will serve; whether the gods which your fathers served that were on the other side of the flood, or the gods of the Amorites, in whose land ye dwell: but as for me and my house, we will serve the LORD."*[19] This is the choice: To follow the One True God or the gods of this world. Anything you place before Almighty God in your life is an idol, a god of this world. Living a godly life, with all the blessings it entails, is pretty simple, but you cannot do it on your own. It

---

[18] Jeremiah 29:11, NASB.
[19] Joshua 24:16.

requires knowing and following God. As Jesus observed, *"With men this is impossible; but with God all things are possible."* So you make the decision!

Living a godly life is synonymous with reading the Holy Bible and following God's plan for your life. And what is His plan for your life?   It is: That you might read, meditate on, and apply Holy Scripture in your life. That you might walk in light, and not in darkness. That you might believe in His Son as your Lord and Saviour, and walk in the way of truth, success, and everlasting life!

<center>~~~~~~~~~~~</center>

"Whether therefore ye eat, or drink, or whatsoever ye do,
do all to the glory of God."
~~~ Psalm 37:23

Chapter 2
All Things Are Possible

~ ~ ~ ~ ~

"But Jesus beheld them, and said unto them, With men this is impossible;
but with God all things are possible."
~~~Matthew 19:26

"This book of the law shall not depart out of thy mouth; but thou shalt meditate
therein day and night, that thou mayest observe to do according to all that is
written therein: for then thou shalt make thy way prosperous,
and then thou shalt have good success."
~~~ Joshua 1:8

"And Jesus looking upon them saith,
With men it is impossible, but not with God:
for with God all things are possible."
~~~ Mark 10:27

~ ~ ~ ~ ~

It is not enough to read the words of this book. They must be understood and applied.

For example, if you were burdened financially, having marital problems, health problems, or trouble with friendships, our tendency would be to preoccupy our time worrying or being anxious. But what does the Word of God say we should do?

In the Book of Philippians, we read:

> [6] Be anxious for nothing, but in everything by prayer and supplication with thanksgiving let your requests be made known to God.

[7] And the peace of God, which surpasses all comprehension, will guard your hearts and your minds in Christ Jesus. [Philippians 4:6-7, NASB]

The power and simplicity of this passage is awesome!

First, we are commanded to *"Be anxious for nothing,"*[20] meaning, we are not to be troubled by the challenges of the day. Remember, 2 Timothy 1:7 tells us, *"For God hath not given us the spirit of fear; but of power, and of love, and of a sound mind."* Being anxious or having fear in our walk is not of God. Anxiousness and fear do nothing to resolve problems or improve your health and other relationships with people. In fact, they hinder us in our walk, and they do nothing positive. On the other hand, being poised or calm of spirit helps us focus and be in tune with our surroundings and our situation. It clears the mind and the heart, and prepares us to properly deal with whatever the troubling matter is.

Secondly, we are to pray to God.[21] This involves speaking directly to God. Yes, the Creator of the universe wants to hear from you! Proverbs 15:8 gives us insight to how the Lord regards this truth, when it states, *"the prayer of the upright is His delight."* And Scripture tells us in 1 Peter 3:12, *"For the eyes of the Lord are over the righteous, and his ears are open unto their prayers."*

Thirdly, we are to make our petition directly to God. Ask Him. Scripture calls this *"supplication."*[22] And in Matthew 21:22, we read, *"And all things, whatsoever ye shall ask in prayer, believing, ye shall receive."* Make your request known to God. As James 4:2 states, *"...ye have not, because ye ask not."* Ask Him!

---

[20] Philippians 4:6, NASB.
[21] Philippians 4:6.
[22] Philippians 4:6.

Finally, we are to thank God, because we know He loves us unconditionally, He is faithful, and He has promised not to forsake[23] us. We are commanded to give thanks in all things. In 1 Thessalonians 5:18 we read, *"In every thing give thanks: for this is the will of God in Christ Jesus concerning you."*

But the real question is: *Will this approach work?* Specifically, will it work for you? The answer is: *Yes!*

Perhaps the most powerful demonstration of this truth is found in the Gospel of John, Chapter 11. Here, Jesus is informed that a friend whom He loved, Lazarus, is sick.[24] And although Lazarus was far off, Jesus was not anxious. In fact, Scripture tells us He tarried where He was for two additional days.[25] This was perplexing to both His disciples and other friends of Lazarus, as they had seen Jesus heal the sick, and they wanted the same for Lazarus.[26]

Note, Jesus was not anxious at the news His friend was sick. He remained where He was for two additional days before journeying to the home of Lazarus. And Jesus knew Lazarus had died.[27]

When He arrived at the home of Lazarus, Jesus proceeded to the gravesite of His friend. Jesus prayed to the Father,[28] having

---

[23] Deuteronomy 4:31, 31:6, 31:8; 1 Chronicles 28:20; Psalm 94:14; Isaiah 41:17.

[24] John 11:3. *"Therefore his sisters sent unto him, saying, Lord, behold, he whom thou lovest is sick."*

[25] John 11:6. *"When he had heard therefore that he was sick, he abode two days still in the same place where he was."*

[26] John 11:37. *"And some of them said, Could not this man, which opened the eyes of the blind, have caused that even this man should not have died?"*

[27] John 11:14. *"Then said Jesus unto them plainly, Lazarus is dead."*

[28] John 11:41. *"Then they took away the stone from the place where the dead was laid. And Jesus lifted up his eyes, and said, Father, I thank thee that thou hast heard me."*

made His supplication for Lazarus to rise again,[29] and gave thanks to God.[30]

It is important to highlight here that this was all done before Lazarus was raised from the dead. It was only after (1) not being anxious, (2) praying, (3) making supplication, and (4) giving thanks to God, that Lazarus was raised from the dead.[31]

In this example, Jesus again sets the standard for living a godly life, and it is here He teaches us how to deal with troubles, regardless of their magnitude. Just as He instructed the disciples on how to pray,[32] Jesus was teaching His followers to live life to its fullest, with power. With God, all things are possible![33]

In Isaiah 41:10, we read:

> [10] Fear not, for I *am* with you; Be not dismayed, for I *am* your God. I will strengthen you, Yes, I will help you, I will uphold you with My righteous right hand.

If we are in His will, He hears us, and He helps us. And if the answer to our prayerful request is not on our timetable, trust that He answers prayers perfectly. Yes, perfectly! He answers prayer at exactly the right time, and we know His remedy for anything that confronts us is infinitely better than any choice we would have made for ourselves on the matter. Now that is awesome!

---

[29] John 11:23. *"Jesus saith unto her, Thy brother shall rise again."*

[30] John 11:41. *"Then they took away the stone from the place where the dead was laid. And Jesus lifted up his eyes, and said, Father, I thank thee that thou hast heard me."*

[31] John 11:43-44. *"And when he thus had spoken, he cried with a loud voice, Lazarus, come forth. And he that was dead came forth, bound hand and foot with graveclothes: and his face was bound about with a napkin. Jesus saith unto them, Loose him, and let him go."*

[32] Matthew 6:9-13.

[33] Philippians 4:13. *"I can do all things through Christ which strengtheneth me."*

~~~~~~~~~

*"For if any be a hearer of the word, and not a
doer, he is like unto a man beholding his
natural face in a glass:
For he beholdeth himself, and goeth his way,
and straightway forgetteth
what manner of man he was."*
~~~ *James 1:23-24.*

Chapter 3
Know These Three Things

~ ~ ~ ~ ~

God Loves You

*"For God so loved the world, that he gave his only begotten Son,
that whosoever believeth in him should not perish, but have everlasting life."*
~~~ John 3:16

God Knows You Better Than You Know Yourself

*"But the very hairs of your head are all numbered.
Fear ye not therefore, ye are of more value than many sparrows."*
~~~ Matthew 10:30-31

*"Before I formed thee in the belly I knew thee;
and before thou camest forth out of the womb I sanctified thee,
and I ordained thee a prophet unto the nations."*
~~~ Jeremiah 1:5

*"'For I know the plans that I have for you,' declares the Lord,
'plans for welfare and not for calamity to give you a future and a hope.'"*
~~~ Jeremiah 29:11, NASB

God Cares About You

"Casting all your care upon him; for he careth for you."
~~~ 1 Peter 5:7

*"But my God shall supply all your need according
to his riches in glory by Christ Jesus."*
~~~ Philippians 4:19

"I will not leave you comfortless: I will come to you."
~~~ John 14:18

~ ~ ~ ~ ~

Perhaps because of my military training, or more likely my insight from the Holy Spirit, I have learned that developing and keeping priorities are essential to success in whatever endeavor we are engaged.

With this in mind, I have learned, and taught others, that keeping our focus on God is essential. While people and things of this world may fail us, God never does. He is our priority. In all things, we must first and foremost focus on God. We do this most effectively when we know these three things: (1) God loves you, (2) He knows you better than you know yourself, and (3) He cares about you! Let us discuss these three things and explain their importance in our lives, especially as we confront challenges on this journey of faith.

(1) **God Loves You!** This is the foundation of our faith, and something we need to know first and foremost. More personally, it is important to understand that God loves You! He made you in His image, with a specific plan and purpose for your life. All throughout Scripture we read about God's unconditional love for His children. One familiar passage so succinctly describes this love, but we often fail to grasp the depth of its meaning. It is the most well-known verse in the Bible:

> [16] For God so loved the world, that he gave his only begotten Son, that whosoever believeth in him should not perish, but have everlasting life. [John 3:16]

God's love is the fountain of all of life's blessings, and we must accept it to live life at its very best. And this love is eternal, as God, the author of love, tells us in Hebrews 13:5, *"I will never leave thee, nor forsake thee."* Jesus tells us in John 14:16-17, *"[16]And I will pray the Father, and he shall give you another Comforter, that he may abide with you for ever; [17]Even the Spirit of truth; whom the world*

30

cannot receive, because it seeth him not, neither knoweth him: but ye know him; for he dwelleth with you, and shall be in you." And if that is not reassuring enough, our Lord goes on in John 14:23 to state, "If a man love me, he will keep my words: and my Father will love him, and we will come unto him, and make our abode with him." God promises that He, the Father, Son, and Holy Spirit, will be in us. He loves us that much! He will never leave or forsake us! Know that God always keeps His promises,[34] as He is absolutely faithful.[35]

(2) **God Knows You Better than You Know Yourself!** As much as we think we know ourselves, God knows us infinitely better. He knew you and me before the foundations of the world,[36] He knows the number of hairs on our head,[37] and He knows our future. Without a doubt, He knows us better than we know ourselves!

God's intimate knowledge of us is a testament to His love for us! The God who brought the very universe into existence[38] also knows the number of hairs on our heads.[39] And He tells us in Jeremiah 1:5, "Before I formed thee in the belly I knew thee." Cast out any doubt, God knows you better than you know yourself.

(3) **God Cares About You!** This is the great promise we can rest all of our hopes on! Jesus tells us in John 14:18 that because He cares about us, "I will not leave you comfortless: I will come to you." This is especially comforting in times of crisis. God cares so much about us that He declares in Isaiah 41:10:

---

[34] Hebrews 10:23, "...for He is faithful that promised."
[35] Deuteronomy 7:9; Psalm 36:5; Isaiah 49:7; 1 John 1:9.
[36] Ephesians 1:4.
[37] Matthew 10:30.
[38] Genesis 1:1.
[39] Matthew 10:30.

> ¹⁰ Fear not, for I *am* with you; Be not
> dismayed, for I *am* your God. I will strengthen
> you, Yes, I will help you, I will uphold you with
> My righteous right hand.

And we are further reassured in Philippians 4:19, when we read, *"...God will supply all your need according to His riches and glory by Christ Jesus."* We can take heart that this is an inexhaustible fulfilment of needs. There is no greater supplier of our needs. Trust Him!

Jeremiah 29:11 puts it all in perspective, *"'For I know the plans that I have for you,' declares the Lord, 'plans for welfare and not for calamity to give you a future and a hope.'"*

And remember this: Jesus said He came so that we, those who believe in Him as Saviour, might have life, and have it more abundantly. As Jesus testified in John 10:10, *"I am come that they might have life, and that they might have it more abundantly."* This is the overflowing goodness and mercy of God. And in Psalm 34:7 God's Word further declares, *"Delight thyself also in the Lord: and he shall give thee the desires of thine heart."* As His children, He promises to care for us and meet all of our needs, and if we would do so little a thing as *"delight"* ourselves in Him, He will also give us the desires of our heart. How great is this mighty assurance?

No matter what befalls you, know this: God is on your side! He loves you, He knows you better than you know yourself, and He cares about you! With this knowledge and understanding, you are in good hands! In fact, you are in the best possible hands. His Word says, in 1 Peter 5:7, *"Casting all your care upon Him; for He careth for you."* With Him, your future is assured,[40] all your needs are met,[41] and all things are possible![42] You can take this journey of faith with trust and confidence in Him. Be of good cheer!

---

[40] Jeremiah 29:11.
[41] Philippians 4:19.
[42] Matthew 19:26.

~~~~~~~~~~

"Thy word is a lamp unto my feet, and a light unto my path."
~~~ Psalm 119:105

Chapter 4
Called for a Purpose

~ ~ ~ ~ ~

"'For I know the plans that I have for you,' declares the Lord,
'plans for welfare and not for calamity to give you a future and a hope.'"
~~~ Jeremiah 29:11, NASB

"And we know that all things work together for good to them that love God,
to them who are the called according to his purpose."
~~~ Romans 8:28

"Trust in the LORD with all thine heart;
and lean not unto thine own understanding.
In all thy ways acknowledge him, and he shall direct thy paths."
~~~ Proverbs 3:5-6

~ ~ ~ ~ ~

If you are human, the simple fact is that you have gone through some difficult times. They are a fact of life. No person in the history of man has gone through life without trials. Even Jesus had difficult times. But the real test is what we do when difficult times befall us. Do we reflect and ask, *"Why me?"* Do we dwell on negative things in an anxious state? After all, we are only human, right?

Well, if I may, might I suggest you are infinitely more than just human? After all, if you are a believer in the Lord Jesus Christ, are you not indwelled by the Father, Son, and Holy Spirit? And is not the Holy Spirit with you to comfort, teach and guide you in this walk of faith?

In John 14:23, *"Jesus answered and said unto him, If a man love me, he will keep my words: and my Father will love him, and we will come unto him, and make our abode with him."* This proves that the Father and the Son live in us. And Jesus went on in John 14:26, *"But the Comforter, which is the Holy Ghost, whom the Father will send in my name, he shall teach you all things, and bring all things to your remembrance, whatsoever I have said unto you."* These are the promises of God. Know them. Dwell on them. And take comfort and strength from them.

You can do all things through God! Philippians 4:13 says, *"I can do all things through Christ which strengtheneth me."* And this is true! But I would like to challenge you to apply it in your life. The Christian does this by declaring, *"I will do all things through Christ who strengthens me!"*

When troubles befall you, turn to God. Ask Him, *"Lord, what are you teaching me through this matter?"* Grow closer to God through your trials. James 4:8 tells us, *"Draw nigh to God, and he will draw nigh to you."* Apply Holy Scripture, like Romans 8:28, which states, *"And we know that all things work together for good to them that love God, to them who are the called according to his purpose."* Note that Scripture says *"All things work together for good,"* not just the pleasant things that come our way. Like it or not, we often learn the most valuable lessons when we stumble or face trial.

And as I mention often in this book, always remember to give thanks to God. No matter what the situation, remember, He has allowed the matter to be brought to your attention for a good purpose. 1 Thessalonians 5:18 commands us, *"In every thing give thanks: for this is the will of God in Christ Jesus concerning you."* Do it! Trust that God is doing a great work in your life. You will be blessed!

Discovering God's plans for your life is important. God knows them, and it does not matter how old you are. In Jeremiah 29:11, we read, *"For I know the plans that I have for you,' declares the Lord, 'plans for welfare and not for calamity to give you a future and a hope."* You should know His plans as well. After all, it is like setting out on an important trip and not knowing your directions or destination. I would certainly hope we would give at least as much attention to God's plans for us as we would to our next planned vacation destination. It only makes sense.

So now we come to the question of the ages: *"What do we do to discover God's direction and plan for our lives?"* This is a great question, because it is like finding ourselves lost in the wilderness at night, with no idea of where we are or where to go. It can be a frightening predicament.

We first need to rely on an authority to solve this problem. Being lost in the forest, for example, we might rely on GPS or a compass and a map. But in navigating life, that is, discovering where we are and where we should go, well, that requires something special. The consequences are too great to leave this to mere chance. And I can think of no better authority or example to follow than that of the Lord Jesus Christ. Jesus was known by those closest to Him as a man of prayer,[43] a man who sought the Father, and read Scripture and applied It, especially when it came to defeating the temptations of the devil.[44] Jesus was intimately familiar with Scripture, even the prophesies that foretold of His coming, from His virgin birth in Bethlehem to His death on the cross, to His resurrection on the third day to His return. Jesus studied and applied Holy Scripture in His life as a human being. He did it, and you can too!

Reading, meditating on, and applying Holy Scripture is key to unlocking God's plans and purpose for your life. You may ask, *"How*

---

[43] Luke 6:12.
[44] Luke 4:2-13.

can one Book, which has been read by billions of people, speak directly to me and my unique circumstances?" It's a good question, and my answer is, the Bible is like a beautiful, captivating piece of fine art. It says something different and wonderful to each and every viewer studying its content. But the Bible is much more than that. It is the most important book ever written, or ever will be written. It is the complete Word of God, what my pastor once called, "the unfolding revelation"[45] of God. You can read a passage of Holy Scripture more than once, and each time you read it you can discover new insight to Its powerful, timeless message. Passages often leap out at me, even after reading them before, because they are applicable to all situations and stages of life. Know in your heart that all of God's Word applies directly to you! The Bible is the key to discovering God's plans and purpose for your life. Psalm 119:105 states it splendidly, "Thy Word is a lamp unto my feet, and a light unto my path." Study it! Use it!

~~~~~~~~~~

"But Jesus beheld them, and said unto them, With men this is impossible; but with God all things are possible."
~~~~Matthew 19:26

---

[45] Dr. Charles F. Stanley, Senior Pastor, First Baptist Church of Atlanta, 2012.

Chapter 5
The Power of Prayer

~ ~ ~ ~ ~

"Pray without ceasing."
~~~ 1 Thessalonians 5:17

"Ye lust, and have not: ye kill, and desire to have, and cannot obtain:
ye fight and war, yet ye have not, because ye ask not."
~~~ James 4:2

"But without faith it is impossible to please him: for he that cometh to God must
believe that he is, and that he is a rewarder of them that diligently seek him."
~~~ Hebrews 11:6

"And the prayer of faith shall save the sick, and the Lord shall raise him up;
and if he have committed sins, they shall be forgiven him.
Confess your faults one to another, and pray one for another,
that ye may be healed.
The effectual fervent prayer of a righteous man availeth much."
~~~ James 5:15-16

"Call unto me, and I will answer thee,
and show thee great and mighty things, which thou knowest not."
~~~ Jeremiah 33:3

"And all things, whatsoever ye shall ask in prayer, believing, ye shall receive."
~~~Matthew 21:22

~ ~ ~ ~ ~

Prayer is powerful! It is life changing and history making! The Holy Bible is replete with example after example on how God moves mightily in response to prayer. In my own life, I can attest to the power of prayer. Time after time after time, God hears our prayers and answers them in an awesome way, never failing to hear our pleas, and truly giving us more than we hoped for or deserved.

These may be prayers for us or intercessory prayers on behalf of loved ones. God hears them all! This is the power of prayer!

God answers prayer even when we fall short in our own walk of faith. One shining example of this is a story in the Bible you might recall from childhood. It is the story of Samson, who was blessed by the Lord.[46] Samson was born during a time the Philistines had dominion over Israel.[47] It was God's plan for Samson that he would *"begin to deliver Israel out of the hand of the Philistines."*[48] And it was at this time the Lord God moved mightily in the life of Samson, so much so that when the Philistines moved to capture him, Judges 15:15 states, *"And he found a new jawbone of an ass, and put forth his hand, and took it, and slew a thousand men therewith."* Samson found favour with the Lord.

But Samson strayed from the safety and strength of God's will in his life when he took up with the Philistines, slept with a harlot, and engaged in an adulterous relationship with a conspirator who sought to betray him for a payment of silver. And betray him she did, as we read in Judges 16:6-21:

> [6] And Delilah said to Samson, Tell me, I pray thee, wherein thy great strength lieth, and wherewith thou mightest be bound to afflict thee.
>
> [7] And Samson said unto her, If they bind me with seven green withs that were never dried, then shall I be weak, and be as another man.
>
> [8] Then the lords of the Philistines brought up to her seven green withs which had not been dried, and she bound him with them.

---

[46] Judges 13:24.
[47] Judges 14:4.
[48] Judges 13:5.

⁹ Now there were men lying in wait, abiding with her in the chamber. And she said unto him, The Philistines be upon thee, Samson. And he brake the withs, as a thread of tow is broken when it toucheth the fire. So his strength was not known.

¹⁰ And Delilah said unto Samson, Behold, thou hast mocked me, and told me lies: now tell me, I pray thee, wherewith thou mightest be bound.

¹¹ And he said unto her, If they bind me fast with new ropes that never were occupied, then shall I be weak, and be as another man.

¹² Delilah therefore took new ropes, and bound him therewith, and said unto him, The Philistines be upon thee, Samson. And there were liers in wait abiding in the chamber. And he brake them from off his arms like a thread.

¹³ And Delilah said unto Samson, Hitherto thou hast mocked me, and told me lies: tell me wherewith thou mightest be bound. And he said unto her, If thou weavest the seven locks of my head with the web.

¹⁴ And she fastened it with the pin, and said unto him, The Philistines be upon thee, Samson. And he awaked out of his sleep, and went away with the pin of the beam, and with the web.

¹⁵ And she said unto him, How canst thou say, I love thee, when thine heart is not with me? thou hast mocked me these three times, and hast not told me wherein thy great strength lieth.

¹⁶ And it came to pass, when she pressed him daily with her words, and urged him, so that his soul was vexed unto death;

^{17} That he told her all his heart, and said unto her, There hath not come a razor upon mine head; for I have been a Nazarite unto God from my mother's womb: if I be shaven, then my strength will go from me, and I shall become weak, and be like any other man.

^{18} And when Delilah saw that he had told her all his heart, she sent and called for the lords of the Philistines, saying, Come up this once, for he hath shewed me all his heart. Then the lords of the Philistines came up unto her, and brought money in their hand.

^{19} And she made him sleep upon her knees; and she called for a man, and she caused him to shave off the seven locks of his head; and she began to afflict him, and his strength went from him.

^{20} And she said, The Philistines be upon thee, Samson. And he awoke out of his sleep, and said, I will go out as at other times before, and shake myself. And he wist not that the LORD was departed from him.

^{21} But the Philistines took him, and put out his eyes, and brought him down to Gaza, and bound him with fetters of brass; and he did grind in the prison house.

And although Samson strayed from God's commandments, and paid dearly for his transgressions, God still loved him. In fact, God would answer Samson's prayer even in the final moments of his mortal life, as we read in the next and final verses of Judges 16:

^{22} Howbeit the hair of his head began to grow again after he was shaven.

²³ Then the lords of the Philistines gathered them together for to offer a great sacrifice unto Dagon their god, and to rejoice: for they said, Our god hath delivered Samson our enemy into our hand.

²⁴ And when the people saw him, they praised their god: for they said, Our god hath delivered into our hands our enemy, and the destroyer of our country, which slew many of us.

²⁵ And it came to pass, when their hearts were merry, that they said, Call for Samson, that he may make us sport. And they called for Samson out of the prison house; and he made them sport: and they set him between the pillars.

²⁶ And Samson said unto the lad that held him by the hand, Suffer me that I may feel the pillars whereupon the house standeth, that I may lean upon them.

²⁷ Now the house was full of men and women; and all the lords of the Philistines were there; and there were upon the roof about three thousand men and women, that beheld while Samson made sport.

²⁸ And Samson called unto the LORD, and said, O Lord God, remember me, I pray thee, and strengthen me, I pray thee, only this once, O God, that I may be at once avenged of the Philistines for my two eyes.

²⁹ And Samson took hold of the two middle pillars upon which the house stood, and on which it was borne up, of the one with his right hand, and of the other with his left.

³⁰ And Samson said, Let me die with the Philistines. And he bowed himself with all his might; and the house fell upon the lords, and upon all the people that were therein. So the dead which he slew at his death were more than they which he slew in his life.

³¹ Then his brethren and all the house of his father came down, and took him, and brought him up, and buried him between Zorah and Eshtaol in the buryingplace of Manoah his father. And he judged Israel twenty years. [Judges 16:22-31]

In his final acts as a man, Samson prayed to God, sought His strength, and destroyed all the lords of the Philistines. This is the power of prayer. On that day, Samson returned to the purpose and plan God had for his life to begin freeing His chosen people from oppression, and killed more of the enemies of the Lord than he had in his entire life. Samson, despite his frailties, loved God. And what was meant for evil by the Philistines was turned into good by God, proving the great truth of Romans 8:28: *"And we know that all things work together for good to them that love God, to them who are the called according to his purpose."*

Prayer opens the door to indescribable peace, understanding, and power. Prayer is our means of direct communication with the Creator of the universe. So pray!

Perhaps one of the most powerful illustrations on the power capable of being unleashed by prayer was found in an encounter in the Garden of Gethsemane. As Jesus was about to be taken by the servants of the high priests and the elders, Peter struck one of the servants of the high priest with a sword. Matthew 26:52-54 records the Lord's response:

⁵² Then said Jesus unto him, Put up again thy sword into his place: for all they that take the sword shall perish with the sword.

⁵³ Thinkest thou that I cannot now pray to my Father, and he shall presently give me more than twelve legions of angels?

⁵⁴ But how then shall the scriptures be fulfilled, that thus it must be?

In these few simple verses, Jesus revealed His destiny was the fulfilment of God's will, that is, to be both God and man and live and die as a substitute for you and me in our sin judgment. And as easy as it would have been for Jesus to avoid His suffering and stop His crucifixion and atonement for our sins, He loved us so much that He suffered the penalty for our transgressions, so that our sins might be forgiven and our relationship with God might be restored, and we might have everlasting life with Him.

Note, Jesus said He could *"now pray to my Father, and he shall presently give me more than twelve legions of angels."* This was a powerful declaration on the ability of prayer to manifest the awesome power of God in our lives. And it was a sobering testament to our Lord's strict adherence to doing the will of God.

The Old Testament is replete with vivid depictions of the awesome, destructive power of angels. In Genesis 19, God sent just two angels to destroy the city of Sodom,[49] and destroy it they did.[50] In 2 Kings 19, when the battle-hardened Assyrian army, led by their king, Sennacherib, surrounded Jerusalem and threatened to utterly destroy God's chosen people, Holy Scripture notes the King of Judah prayed to the Lord.[51] Verse 19 records the words of Hezekiah, King of Judah, *"Now therefore, O LORD our God, I beseech thee, save thou us out of his hand, that all the kingdoms of the earth may know that thou art the LORD God, even thou only."* God answered that prayer and sent a single angel that night, which killed 185,000 Assyrians.

---

[49] Genesis 19:13.
[50] Genesis 19: 24-25.
[51] 2 Kings 19:15.

2 Kings 19:35 records the carnage, *"And it came to pass that night, that the angel of the L*ORD *went out, and smote in the camp of the Assyrians an hundred fourscore and five thousand: and when they arose early in the morning, behold, they were all dead corpses."*

It suffices knowing that if one angel could lay waste to 185,000 Assyrian soldiers on one given night, just imagine what the *"twelve legions of angels"* that Jesus spoke of could have done. Understand a single legion of angels would be the numerical equivalent of a Roman legion of 3,000 to 6,000 soldiers. That would make the force Jesus spoke of anywhere between 36,000 to 72,000 angels. Such a force the world has never known. It could lay waste to the entire planet, even today. These are testaments to the power of prayer and the compassion and love of God.

A knowledge and understanding of prayer would be incomplete without knowing what Jesus Himself said about the subject. In Matthew 6:5-18, Christ Jesus shares with us how to pray and where to pray, and He speaks on the subject of fasting as well:

> [5] And when thou prayest, thou shalt not be as the hypocrites are: for they love to pray standing in the synagogues and in the corners of the streets, that they may be seen of men. Verily I say unto you, They have their reward.
>
> [6] But thou, when thou prayest, enter into thy closet, and when thou hast shut thy door, pray to thy Father which is in secret; and thy Father which seeth in secret shall reward thee openly.
>
> [7] But when ye pray, use not vain repetitions, as the heathen do: for they think that they shall be heard for their much speaking.
>
> [8] Be not ye therefore like unto them: for your Father knoweth what things ye have need of, before ye ask him.

[9] After this manner therefore pray ye: Our Father which art in heaven, Hallowed be thy name.

[10] Thy kingdom come, Thy will be done in earth, as it is in heaven.

[11] Give us this day our daily bread.

[12] And forgive us our debts, as we forgive our debtors.

[13] And lead us not into temptation, but deliver us from evil: For thine is the kingdom, and the power, and the glory, for ever. Amen.

[14] For if ye forgive men their trespasses, your heavenly Father will also forgive you:

[15] But if ye forgive not men their trespasses, neither will your Father forgive your trespasses.

[16] Moreover when ye fast, be not, as the hypocrites, of a sad countenance: for they disfigure their faces, that they may appear unto men to fast. Verily I say unto you, They have their reward.

[17] But thou, when thou fastest, anoint thine head, and wash thy face;

[18] That thou appear not unto men to fast, but unto thy Father which is in secret: and thy Father, which seeth in secret, shall reward thee openly.

In these few but powerful passages, Jesus shares the purpose, nature, and power of prayer. First, prayer is a private, personal communication with Almighty God. It begins with an acknowledgement that He is Holy, and the Lord of our lives and of the entire universe. We are then instructed to make supplication, that is, to request His provision for our lives, which is a petition for all that we need to accomplish His goal for our lives. Next, we are instructed to seek forgiveness from God for any transgressions, to the same degree we forgive others who have offended us. This is not only a blessing to us, but a blessing to others. In this respect, we reap what we sow, knowing this is the will of our heavenly Father. And finally, Jesus instructs us to seek God's protection from the wiles of the devil, that is, to show us favour and lead us in a godly walk, keeping us from all things evil.

Toward the conclusion of the Lord's Prayer (Matthew 6:9-13), we note the importance of asking God to deliver us from evil. And by no coincidence, this was our Lord's earthly ministry: Jesus delivered the oppressed from evil. On one occasion, the apostles were ministering in the manner of Christ, but were unable to expel the devil from a child they encountered. Seeing this thing, Jesus rebuked the devil, and cast him out of the child;[52] when the apostles asked Him why they could not cast out the devil,[53] Jesus shared the power of prayer, combined with fasting, and declared in Matthew 17:21, *"Howbeit this kind goeth not out but by prayer and fasting."* This is why Jesus also instructs us in fasting in Matthew 6:16-18. Prayer and fasting are an essential part of our walk as Christians.

And in all things, including prayer and fasting, we are to give thanks to God for the great privilege of being His children, a part of His kingdom, and as such the recipients of His grace and His power and His glory. As *1 Thessalonians 5:18* states, *"In every thing give thanks: for this is the will of God in Christ Jesus concerning you."* So give God thanks!

Prayer is powerful. Godly men have known this throughout history. And the important thing to remember is that people may

---

[52] Matthew 17:18.
[53] Matthew 17:19.

change, but God never changes. He is the same yesterday, today, and tomorrow. He is faithful, and longs for an intimate relationship with each and every one of us. This is why He sent His Son! He hears and answers our prayers. What an awesome blessing!

Dr. Jerry Falwell once told me something that Chrysostom, an early church father in the latter days of the Roman Empire, had said about the power of prayer. This quote had *"great meaning"* to Dr. Falwell:[54]

> The potency of prayer hath subdued the strength of fire; it hath bridled the rage of lions, hushed anarchy to rest, extinguished wars, appeased the elements, expelled demons, burst the chains of death, expanded the gates of heaven, assuaged diseases, repelled frauds, rescued cities from destruction, stayed the sun in its course, and arrested the progress of the thunderbolt.
>
> *~~~John Chrysostom, 349-407 A.D., born in Antioch, and considered an important early church father. He ministered during the time of the Roman Emperor Theodosius I. Chrysostom was Archbishop of Constantinople, who served under Pope Innocent I, and was venerated as a saint soon after his death. The Orthodox and Eastern Catholic Churches honor him as a saint.*

How true! Prayer has done all these things and more! Such is the power of prayer! What was true about God yesterday is true today. God loves you, He hears you, and He answers prayer! So pray!

---

[54] Dr. Jerry Falwell, at Thomas Road Baptist Church, Lynchburg, Virginia, September 12, 1993.

~~~~~~~~~~

"Call unto me, and I will answer thee,
and show thee great and mighty things, which thou knowest not."
~~~ Jeremiah 33:3

Chapter 6
Foundations of the Faith

~ ~ ~ ~ ~

"In the beginning was the Word,
and the Word was with God, and the Word was God."
~~~ John 1:1

"Thy word is a lamp unto my feet, and a light unto my path."
~~~ Psalm 119:105

"Enter ye in at the strait gate: for wide is the gate, and broad is the way,
that leadeth to destruction, and many there be which go in thereat:
Because strait is the gate, and narrow is the way, which leadeth unto life,
and few there be that find it."
~~~ Matthew 7:13-14

"For God so loved the world, that he gave his only begotten Son,
that whosoever believeth in him should not perish, but have everlasting life."
~~~ John 3:16

"For the preaching of the cross is to them that perish foolishness;
but unto us which are saved it is the power of God."
~~~ 1 Corinthians 1:18

"Then one of them, which was a lawyer, asked him a question, tempting him, and
saying, Master, which is the great commandment in the law? Jesus said unto him,
Thou shalt love the Lord thy God with all thy heart, and with all thy soul, and with
all thy mind. This is the first and great commandment.
And the second is like unto it, Thou shalt love thy neighbour as thyself.
On these two commandments hang all the law and the prophets."
~~~ Matthew 22:35-40

"This book of the law shall not depart out of thy mouth; but thou shalt meditate
therein day and night, that thou mayest observe to do according to all that is
written therein: for then thou shalt make thy way prosperous,
and then thou shalt have good success."
~~~ Joshua 1:8

"But my God shall supply all your need
According to his riches in glory by Christ Jesus."
~~~ Philippians 4:19

"Let us hear the conclusion of the whole matter:
Fear God, and keep his commandments: for this is the whole duty of man."
~~~ Ecclesiastes 12:13

~ ~ ~ ~ ~

Let's face it: We live in a corrupt world. The Word of God is cast aside for selfish desires and political correctness. We condone same-sex marriage, the murder of our unborn children, and when it comes down to it, many who call themselves *"believers"* prefer to follow their feelings than obey God's Word. With this said, we should resolutely heed the admonition of God in Isaiah 5:20, *"Woe unto them that call evil good, and good evil; that put darkness for light, and light for darkness; that put bitter for sweet, and sweet for bitter!"*

The truth is: People change, but God does not! He is the same yesterday, today, and tomorrow. And the beauty of the Holy Bible is that we can actually see God at work in it: His presence in the history of man, His nature and abilities, His unconditional love, His mercy, His grace, His omnipresence, His omnipotence, His will for our lives, His promises, and His commandments. God is real!

God is the foundation of our faith, our hope, our love, and our very existence. And He reveals the nature of this foundation for His children in Ephesians 2:19-22:

> [19] Now therefore ye are no more strangers and foreigners, but fellowcitizens with the saints, and of the household of God;
>
> [20] And are built upon the foundation of the apostles and prophets, Jesus Christ himself being the chief corner stone;

²¹ In whom all the building fitly framed together groweth unto an holy temple in the Lord:

²² In whom ye also are builded together for an habitation of God through the Spirit.

This is the foundation of our faith. We *are "of the household of God."*[55] And the Lord Jesus Christ is the *"chief corner stone"*[56] of this foundation. Thus, any good to come of this book is based on your relationship with God. It is not just an understanding, it is an acceptance of Jesus as Lord and our Saviour, and our surrender to His will. This is the key to personal growth and the way to a successful life.

I began this chapter, and every chapter of this book, with verses of Holy Scripture. They inspire. They edify. They lift the spirit! And as powerful as they are, they only scratch the surface of the world of wonder and enlightenment that awaits you in the Word of God! Seize this moment to dedicate a portion of each and every day to the study of Holy Scripture. Learn the ways of God and His plan for you and your success, and how you can achieve it. It is that simple! Do it!

I have heard it said, *"I barely have time to read the Bible once a week, let alone every day!"* To that, I respectfully say, *"Nonsense!"* If you do not have time to read the Word of God each and every day, then I suggest you are not wisely using your time. I cannot imagine starting each day without reading the Holy Bible, and seeing God's plan for my walk that day. And I would not feel at ease going to sleep each night without hearing the Word of God, and meditating on that Truth before and during my slumber. Psalm 119:105 states, *"Thy word is a lamp unto my feet, and a light unto my path."* I prefer to walk in His light. How about you?

---

[55] Ephesians 2:19.
[56] Ephesians 2:20.

If you believe that you can do without the Word of God in your daily walk, then I suggest you are too arrogant. If you feel like you do not need to know the will of God, and you can do it alone, then you are too prideful. But whether you are too arrogant, prideful, or just plain foolish, you are a mere phone call away from disaster, and a heartbeat away from eternity. I humbly suggest you re-evaluate your walk.

The Word of God is the ultimate authority on the Kingdom of God and the foundation for living a godly life. Read it, and apply it to your life!

Repent! And seek the Kingdom of God!

~~~~~~~~~~

"This book of the law shall not depart out of thy mouth; but thou shalt meditate therein day and night, that thou mayest observe to do according to all that is written therein: for then thou shalt make thy way prosperous, and then thou shalt have good success."
~~~ Joshua 1:8

Chapter 7
The Greatest of These

~ ~ ~ ~ ~

*"If I speak with the tongues of men and of angels, but do not have love,
I have become a noisy gong or a clanging cymbal. If I have the gift of prophecy,
and know all mysteries and all knowledge; and if I have all faith, so as to remove
mountains, but do not have love, I am nothing. And if I give all my possessions to
feed the poor, and if I surrender my body to be burned,
but do not have love, it profits me nothing.*

*Love is patient, love is kind and is not jealous; love does not brag and is not
arrogant, does not act unbecomingly; it does not seek its own, is not provoked,
does not take into account a wrong suffered, does not rejoice in unrighteousness,
but rejoices with the truth; bears all things, believes all things, hopes all things,
endures all things.*

*Love never fails; but if there are gifts of prophecy, they will be done away;
if there are tongues, they will cease; if there is knowledge, it will be done away.*

But now faith, hope, love, abide these three; but the greatest of these is love."
~~~ 1 Corinthians 13:1-8, 13, NASB

~ ~ ~ ~ ~

Love is a gift from God. It is the realization that the Creator of the universe genuinely cares about you and your welfare. His greatest priority for your life is for you to come to a personal relationship with Him.[57] It is the reason He created man, and it is the reason why He created you! It is the reason He sent His only begotten Son, even after man had sinned and turned his back on Him, so you and I could have a restored relationship with God the

---

[57] Stanley, C.F. (2008). *30 Life Principles*. Atlanta: In Touch Ministries.

Father. It is the new and everlasting covenant that creates an unbreakable, unshakeable bond with God.

In 1 John 4:16, we read *"God is love."* But let us explore the qualities of Love, which after all are the qualities of God. 1 Corinthians 13:4-8 [NASB] tells us, *"⁴ Love is **patient**, love is **kind** and is **not jealous**; love **does not brag** and **is not arrogant**, ⁵ does not act unbecomingly; it does not seek its own, is not provoked, does not take into account a wrong suffered, ⁶ does not rejoice in unrighteousness, but rejoices with the truth; ⁷ bears all things, believes all things, hopes all things, endures all things. ⁸ Love never fails."* Know these things, meditate on them, and live them!

Knowing these qualities is important for several reasons, but the primary reasons are (1) God gives us this insight into His nature in His Word, and (2) we are told by the apostle Paul, in Romans 8:29, *"to be conformed to the image of His Son."* This means God is sharing His qualities with us because it is important to Him that we know what being a disciple of His Son entails, or He would not have revealed this to us in His Word. It means living a life that is patient, kind, not jealous, without bragging or arrogance, nor acting unbecoming, it is thinking of others, not being provoked, and keeping no record of wrongs committed against you by loved ones, especially family members, or even your spouse; it means forgiveness. It means rejoicing in the things of God, and not those things that are evil. It means bearing all things, believing in all the promises of God, hoping all things, and enduring all things. It means understanding that God, who is Love, never fails! I say again: God never fails! Count on it! Love is indispensable, and the key to living a godly life!

Furthermore, 1 John 4:16-21 addresses the meaning of love and its presence in our lives. Commit yourself to understanding these precepts. They are important to God, and as such, should be important to us:

¹⁶ And we have known and believed the love that God hath to us. God is love; and he that dwelleth in love dwelleth in God, and God in him.

¹⁷ Herein is our love made perfect, that we may have boldness in the day of judgment: because as he is, so are we in this world.

¹⁸ There is no fear in love; but perfect love casteth out fear: because fear hath torment.

¹⁹ He that feareth is not made perfect in love. We love him, because he first loved us.

²⁰ If a man say, I love God, and hateth his brother, he is a liar: for he that loveth not his brother whom he hath seen, how can he love God whom he hath not seen?

²¹ And this commandment have we from him, That he who loveth God love his brother also.

This is a powerful testament, as it assures us that if we dwell in love, we dwell in God, and God dwells in us. It is a theme we read throughout the New Testament, that is, God abides in those who believe on His Son for their salvation. It is the great hope and promise of our faith. You need never fear when God abides in you.[58] He reassures use that *"perfect love casteth out fear,"* and points to the evidence of the strength of His love, especially when He states, *"he who loveth God love his brother also."* This is the depth and breadth and power of Love in our lives! Jesus loves us unconditionally, and we are to conform to His image and love our neighbors.

---

[58] John 14:16, 23.

There is a difference when we have God in our lives. Man without God cannot love unconditionally. We hate at the slightest provocation. But God loves us unconditionally, no matter what we do. Man is limited. God is all powerful. Having God in our lives changes everything. This is why Jesus said in Matthew 19:26, *"With men this is impossible; but with God all things are possible."* This is the power of God in our lives!

And if you were wondering why God ranked Love above Faith and Hope,[59] think about it. God is love,[60] and existed before the foundations of the world,[61] and even past the end of this age.[62] Faith and hope, on the other hand, really won't exist in the end, because, as 1 John 3:2 declares, *"Beloved, now are we the sons of God, and it doth not yet appear what we shall be: but we know that, when He shall appear, we shall be like Him; for we shall see Him as He is."* All of our faith and hope will then be fulfilled, and we will dwell for an eternity in Love. This is the promise of God. Believe it!

~~~~~~~~~~

"But now faith, hope, love, abide these three;
but the greatest of these is love."
~~~ 1 Corinthians 13:13, NASB

---

[59] 1 Corinthians 13:13.
[60] 1 John 4:16.
[61] John 17:24.
[62] Matthew 28:20.

Chapter 8
Fruit of the Spirit

~ ~ ~ ~ ~

"But the fruit of the Spirit is love, joy, peace, patience, kindness, goodness, faithfulness, gentleness, self-control; against such things there is no law."
~~~ *Galatians 5:22-23, NASB*

"So God created man in his own image, in the image of God created he him; male and female created he them. And God blessed them, and God said unto them, Be fruitful, and multiply, and replenish the earth, and subdue it: and have dominion over the fish of the sea, and over the fowl of the air, and over every living thing that moveth upon the earth."
~~~ *Genesis 1:27-28*

~ ~ ~ ~ ~

In my own walk of faith, I have on occasion heard people say, *"I'm not sure if I'm saved."* And these words are always spoken with a great deal of emotion. In fact, I have heard these words uttered by many people, including people who profess to know Christ. It is a question of uncertainty that deserves a wise answer, an answer based on what the Word of God says.

When a man or woman believes and accepts the fact that Jesus Christ is Lord and came in the flesh and lived among us, and died on the cross, as our substitutionary sacrificial intercessor,[63] and rose again[64] so our relationship with God could be restored, we are *"saved"* and *"born again."* This saving event or *"salvation"* brings us into a personal relationship with the Lord, with the promise of God that the Holy Spirit will indwell us from that point in our walk,

---

[63] 1 John 4:10: *"Herein is love, not that we loved God, but that he loved us, and sent his Son to be the propitiation for our sins."*
[64] Romans 10:9.

and we will have eternal life with God. As Romans 6:23 states, *"For the wages of sin is death; but the gift of God is eternal life through Jesus Christ our Lord."* And Scripture gives us evidence of this salvation in the life of a person:

> [16] Ye shall know them by their fruits. Do men gather grapes of thorns, or figs of thistles?
>
> [17] Even so every good tree bringeth forth good fruit; but a corrupt tree bringeth forth evil fruit.
>
> [18] A good tree cannot bring forth evil fruit, neither can a corrupt tree bring forth good fruit.
>
> [19] Every tree that bringeth not forth good fruit is hewn down, and cast into the fire.
>
> [20] Wherefore by their fruits ye shall know them. [Matthew 7:16-20]

This *"good fruit"* is from God, as He is the source of all that is *"good."*[65] Thus, *"good"* in man comes from God, and is manifested in the life of the Christian through the *"Fruit of the Spirit,"* which Galatians 5:22-23 defines as *"love, joy, peace, patience, kindness, goodness, faithfulness, gentleness, [and] self-control."* Those who are saved have these fruits through the indwelling of the Holy Spirit. But it is important to understand that these fruit grow as we grow in our personal relationship with the Lord. Being impatient does not mean you are not saved. It may just mean that this fruit will develop as your walk in faith develops. Remember, you may possess more gentleness than patience, or vice versa. No two people are the same, but for Christians, the Spirit that dwells within us is the same.[66] And we complement one another as Christians in

---

[65] Mark 10:18; Psalm 106:1; Psalm 118:1; Psalm 118:29; Psalm 119:68; Psalm 136:1; Proverbs 4:2.
[66] 1 Corinthians 12:4-13.

the body of Christ.[67] Each bearing good fruit as the Spirit moves to feed the body of believers all to the glory of God.

I find no option in Holy Scripture for followers of Christ not to be fruitful. All disciples of Christ are commanded to be fruitful, without exception. We are repeatedly commanded by Holy Scripture to be fruitful.[68] Jesus spoke with particular clarity on this in the city of Bethany, when He used a particular fig tree as a metaphor for the absence of spiritual fruit. *"And when he saw a fig tree in the way, he came to it, and found nothing thereon, but leaves only, and said unto it, Let no fruit grow on thee henceforward for ever,"* said the Lord in Matthew 21:19, *"And presently the fig tree withered away."* A fig tree is cultivated for its fruit, which is the edible fig. This is why they are grown. It is a blessing to the hungry. If a fig tree does not bear good fruit and serve the purpose of its existence, it is useless. As Luke 6:44 states, *"For every tree is known by his own fruit. For of thorns men do not gather figs, nor of a bramble bush gather they grapes."*

But there is a staunch warning for us in Matthew 7:17 about fruit, *"Even so every good tree bringeth forth good fruit; but a corrupt tree bringeth forth evil fruit."* The truth is: there is evil fruit, and that fruit is not of God, but is the way of destruction. As Matthew 7:21-27 notes:

> [21] Not every one that saith unto me, Lord, Lord, shall enter into the kingdom of heaven; but he that doeth the will of my Father which is in heaven.

> [22] Many will say to me in that day, Lord, Lord, have we not prophesied in thy name? and in thy name have cast out devils? and in thy name done many wonderful works?

---

[67] 1 Corinthians 12:14-27.
[68] Genesis 1:28; Genesis 9:1.

²³ And then will I profess unto them, I never knew you: depart from me, ye that work iniquity.

²⁴ Therefore whosoever heareth these sayings of mine, and doeth them, I will liken him unto a wise man, which built his house upon a rock:

²⁵ And the rain descended, and the floods came, and the winds blew, and beat upon that house; and it fell not: for it was founded upon a rock.

²⁶ And every one that heareth these sayings of mine, and doeth them not, shall be likened unto a foolish man, which built his house upon the sand:

²⁷ And the rain descended, and the floods came, and the winds blew, and beat upon that house; and it fell: and great was the fall of it.

Evil fruit is a threat to the Christian, and as such the body of Christ. It seeks to spread false doctrine. Its goal is to keep us from knowing and doing the will of God, and fulfilling the purpose of our lives, as it fosters spiritual deception and accusation. It was prevalent in the early church and it is here today. This is why we need to walk about with the Whole Armour of God. Knowing Holy Scripture makes us discerning of the wiles of the devil.

We are taught in Holy Scripture to test the spirits to know whether they are of God. This is done by knowing the Word of God, and comparing what It says to that which we are told. There are many false doctrines, but only one true Word of God. If someone, no matter who that person is, tells us something contrary to the Word of God, we are not to believe them or do as they might ask on the matter. Knowing what God says is critical to our success. Only then can you walk with authority in the Word of God.

1 John 4:1-6 states the following about testing the spirits and knowing who we are in the plan of God:

> [1] Beloved, believe not every spirit, but try the spirits whether they are of God: because many false prophets are gone out into the world.
>
> [2] Hereby know ye the Spirit of God: Every spirit that confesseth that Jesus Christ is come in the flesh is of God:
>
> [3] And every spirit that confesseth not that Jesus Christ is come in the flesh is not of God: and this is that spirit of antichrist, whereof ye have heard that it should come; and even now already is it in the world.
>
> [4] Ye are of God, little children, and have overcome them: because greater is he that is in you, than he that is in the world.
>
> [5] They are of the world: therefore speak they of the world, and the world heareth them.
>
> [6] We are of God: he that knoweth God heareth us; he that is not of God heareth not us. Hereby know we the spirit of truth, and the spirit of error.

Always be on guard with what others tell you the Bible says. Read it for yourself! The Holy Spirit will guide you, and teach you on the things of God, and enable you to bear good fruit. You will discover Truth, discernment, and power. As Christ Jesus assures us in John 15:16, *"I have chosen you, and ordained you, that ye should go and bring forth fruit, and that your fruit should remain: that whatsoever ye shall ask of the Father in my name, he may give it you."*

~~~~~~~~~

"But the fruit of the Spirit is love, joy, peace, patience, kindness, goodness, faithfulness, gentleness, self-control; against such things there is no law."
~~~ Galatians 5:22-23, NASB

Chapter 9
Dwell on These Things

"Finally, brethren, whatever is true, whatever is honorable, whatever is right, whatever is pure, whatever is lovely, whatever is of good repute, if there is any excellence and if anything worthy of praise, dwell on these things."
~~~ Philippians 4:8, NASB

In Psalm 143:10 we read, *"Teach me to do thy will; for thou art my God: thy spirit is good; lead me into the land of uprightness."* That is what the Word of God does: It teaches us about God's will for our lives. And it does not take long for every follower of Christ to see the will of God for him or her in Holy Scripture.

The opening verse of Holy Scripture for this chapter points the way for every Christian toward a positive and godly path. It tells us to *"dwell"* on *"honorable"* and *"right"* and *"pure"* and *"lovely"* things, not on dishonorable, wrong, dark, or hateful things. We are encouraged to lift that which is *"good"* and *"excellent,"* not to promote evil or praise foolishness. This is in keeping with our character as followers of Christ, always conforming to His image.

Understand, there are consequences to not dwelling on good things. And the primary consequences are (1) breaking fellowship with God, in that, while He still loves you unconditionally, you have chosen not to obey His command that we *"dwell on these things;"*[69] (2) developing anxiety, depression, guilt, and hostility, which causes us to deviate from the will of God and lose friendships and our sense of purpose; and (3) it opens the door to satan having a

---

[69] Philippians 4:8, NASB.

stronghold in our lives, which hinders our personal growth and blocks the path to a successful life.

Satan uses the strongholds he obtains in people. Guilt is just one of his weapons. Never listen to, or follow the directions of, someone who says, *"If you love me, you will do this ...,"* especially if it is contrary to the Word of God. This is someone attempting to plant the seeds of guilt in your life, or exploit them if they are already there! Resist the wiles of the devil. Nothing that violates Holy Scripture is from God.

1 Peter 5:8 warns us that *"your adversary the devil, as a roaring lion, walketh about, seeking whom he may devour."* And in his arsenal of weapons, he uses lies, deceit, anxiety, and guilt. He tries to tell us that God doesn't love us, or we are not good enough for God's love. He wants us to dwell on things that are not of God. The devil would have us dwell on the wrong things.

We have all done things in our lives that we regret, wrong things, evil things, but God tells us to *"repent,"*[70] that is, change direction. Jesus assures us that we are *"new creatures"*[71] in and through Him. As it is written in 1 Corinthians 5:17, *"Therefore if any man be in Christ, he is a new creature: old things are passed away; behold, all things are become new."* Satan would have us believe we need to feel guilty, as if our sin debt was not paid in full by Christ Jesus at the cross. Satan's goal is to hinder us, and distract us from our God-given mission. Christ absolutely paid our sin debt in full! We are children of God, washed white as snow, meaning free from sin and guilt, by the atoning blood of His Son.[72]

Be on guard against the wiles of the devil. He would have us embrace guilt and walk in his ungodly will. Stay clear from it! Cling

---

[70] Matthew 4:17; Matthew 9:13; Mark 1:15; Mark 2:17; Luke 5:32; Luke 13:3, 5; Luke 17:3, 4; Revelation 2:5, 16; Revelation 3:3, 19.
[71] 1 Corinthians 5:17.
[72] Matthew 26:28; Mark 14:24; Luke 22:20.

to God, and dwell on good things!

All too often, we hear the voices of our age promoting things that are not honorable, or right, or pure, or lovely. It is these voices which praise the vilest of figures in our society. They champion lewd and violent behavior in their songs and conduct. They are the workers of iniquity. *"²²Professing themselves to be wise, they became fools,"* states Romans 1:22-23, *"²³And changed the glory of the uncorruptible God into an image made like to corruptible man, and to birds, and fourfooted beasts, and creeping things."*

And the most alarming part of being among these voices of our age is their future. Note what Romans 1:24-32 says of them:

> ²⁴ Wherefore God also gave them up to uncleanness through the lusts of their own hearts, to dishonour their own bodies between themselves:
>
> ²⁵ Who changed the truth of God into a lie, and worshipped and served the creature more than the Creator, who is blessed for ever. Amen.
>
> ²⁶ For this cause God gave them up unto vile affections: for even their women did change the natural use into that which is against nature:
>
> ²⁷ And likewise also the men, leaving the natural use of the woman, burned in their lust one toward another; men with men working that which is unseemly, and receiving in themselves that recompence of their error which was meet.
>
> ²⁸ And even as they did not like to retain God in their knowledge, God gave them over to a reprobate mind, to do those things which are not convenient;

^{29} Being filled with all unrighteousness, fornication, wickedness, covetousness, maliciousness; full of envy, murder, debate, deceit, malignity; whisperers,

^{30} Backbiters, haters of God, despiteful, proud, boasters, inventors of evil things, disobedient to parents,

^{31} Without understanding, covenantbreakers, without natural affection, implacable, unmerciful:

^{32} Who knowing the judgment of God, that they which commit such things are worthy of death, not only do the same, but have pleasure in them that do them.

It is a sad future, but remember, with God all things are possible.[73] God has given us the answer to all negativity: His Son! Jesus died a substitutionary death for our sins -- past, present and future -- so that we might have life, and have it more abundantly. We are to repent, that is, turn away from dwelling on the wrong things and turn to dwelling on good, and trust He will handle the rest. Take your concerns to God! This is achieving peace of mind with God and living life at its very best!

~~~~~~~~~~

"Trust in the LORD with all thine heart;
and lean not unto thine own understanding.
In all thy ways acknowledge him, and he shall direct thy paths."
~~~ Proverbs 3:5-6

---

[73] Matthew 19:26.

Chapter 10
The Whole Armour of God

~ ~ ~ ~ ~

"Finally, my brethren, be strong in the Lord, and in the power of his might.
Put on the whole armour of God,
that ye may be able to stand against the wiles of the devil.
For we wrestle not against flesh and blood, but against principalities,
against powers, against the rulers of the darkness of this world,
against spiritual wickedness in high places.
Wherefore take unto you the whole armour of God,
that ye may be able to withstand in the evil day, and having done all, to stand.
Stand therefore, having your loins girt about with truth,
and having on the breastplate of righteousness;
And your feet shod with the preparation of the gospel of peace;
Above all, taking the shield of faith, wherewith ye shall be able to quench all the
fiery darts of the wicked.
And take the helmet of salvation, and the sword of the Spirit,
which is the word of God:
Praying always with all prayer and supplication in the Spirit,
and watching thereunto with all perseverance and supplication for all saints;
And for me, that utterance may be given unto me,
that I may open my mouth boldly,
to make known the mystery of the gospel,
For which I am an ambassador in bonds:
that therein I may speak boldly, as I ought to speak."
~~~ Ephesians 6:10-20

~ ~ ~ ~ ~

I have heard life called a *"struggle."* One acquaintance went so far as to call it being in a state of *"war!"* He described it as, *"a seemingly endless series of crises, occasionally interrupted by boredom."* And this was from the mouth of a successful man by worldly standards. He had money, notoriety, a big home, and an expensive car, but he was missing something in his life. Can you guess what it is?

If you have been reading this book thus far and haven't figured out he was missing the presence of God in his life, then I have done a poor job of presenting the Good News of the Gospel and the power of God in our lives. Of course, he was missing that which gives our life meaning, purpose, direction, and hope: the Lord Jesus Christ. And that, my friends, is a sad existence. It is not only a sad earthly existence, but an eternal death sentence. There is just no easy way to put this: Without the Lord Jesus Christ, you are separated from God and doomed to an eternity in hell. This is the sad truth of it all! But as you may have gathered through your reading, I prefer to dwell on good things!

2 Corinthians 4:8-12, describes a battle field:

> [8] We are troubled on every side, yet not distressed; we are perplexed, but not in despair;
>
> [9] Persecuted, but not forsaken; cast down, but not destroyed;
>
> [10] Always bearing about in the body the dying of the Lord Jesus, that the life also of Jesus might be made manifest in our body.
>
> [11] For we which live are always delivered unto death for Jesus' sake, that the life also of Jesus might be made manifest in our mortal flesh.
>
> [12] So then death worketh in us, but life in you.

The Christian has awesome assurances from God. *"Who shall separate us from the love of Christ?"* asks the apostle Paul in Romans 8:35, *"shall tribulation, or distress, or persecution, or famine, or nakedness, or peril, or sword?"*

Well, Paul goes on to answer that question in Romans 8:37, *"Nay, in all these things we are more than conquerors through him* that loved us." Think about that: *"We are more than conquerors through [Christ Jesus]."* This is the power of God!

And he shares the absolute bond of the Christian to the Lord Jesus Christ in the following two verses (Romans 8:38-39): *"[38]For I am persuaded, that neither death, nor life, nor angels, nor principalities, nor powers, nor things present, nor things to come, [39]Nor height, nor depth, nor any other creature, shall be able to separate us from the love of God, which is in Christ Jesus our Lord."* Now that is blessed assurance!

But what about those who might rise against us in our walk of faith? What about those who might falsely accuse us? Or seek our destruction? What about those who might work evil against us?

By no coincidence, Holy Scripture has an answer to these questions as well: *"No weapon that is formed against thee shall prosper; and every tongue that shall rise against thee in judgment thou shalt condemn,"* declares Isaiah 54:17, *"This is the heritage of the servants of the LORD, and their righteousness is of me, saith the LORD."* Those who believe on the Lord dwell under His protection. Proverbs 30:5 notes, *"Every word of God is pure; He is a shield unto them that put their trust in Him."* This is but a glimpse into the love and protection of Almighty God in the lives of His followers.

And if that was not enough, Psalm 84:11 states, *"For the LORD God is a sun and shield: the LORD will give grace and glory: no good thing will he withhold from them that walk uprightly."* This is not only protection, but favour and direction from God. These are daily blessings!

This direction from God in walking uprightly is shared by the apostle Paul in his first epistle to the church in Thessalonica [1 Thessalonians 5:5-24]. In one of his earliest writings, around the years 51-52 A.D., Paul exhorts us to godly conduct. He shares practical instruction in living a godly life, and introduces fellow-Christians to the Armour of God,[74] namely the Helmet of Salvation[75] and the Breastplate of Righteousness.[76]

> [5] Ye are all the children of light, and the children of the day: we are not of the night, nor of darkness.
>
> [6] Therefore let us not sleep, as do others; but let us watch and be sober.
>
> [7] For they that sleep sleep in the night; and they that be drunken are drunken in the night.
>
> [8] But let us, who are of the day, be sober, putting on the breastplate of faith and love; and for an helmet, the hope of salvation.
>
> [9] For God hath not appointed us to wrath, but to obtain salvation by our Lord Jesus Christ,
>
> [10] Who died for us, that, whether we wake or sleep, we should live together with him.
>
> [11] Wherefore comfort yourselves together, and edify one another, even as also ye do.
>
> [12] And we beseech you, brethren, to know them which labour among you, and are over you in the Lord, and admonish you;
>
> [13] And to esteem them very highly in love for their work's sake. And be at peace among yourselves.
>
> [14] Now we exhort you, brethren, warn them that are unruly, comfort the feebleminded, support the weak, be patient toward all men.

---

[74] Ephesians 6:11.
[75] Ephesians 6:17.
[76] Ephesians 6:14.

[15] See that none render evil for evil unto any man; but ever follow that which is good, both among yourselves, and to all men.

[16] Rejoice evermore.

[17] Pray without ceasing.

[18] In every thing give thanks: for this is the will of God in Christ Jesus concerning you.

[19] Quench not the Spirit.

[20] Despise not prophesyings.

[21] Prove all things; hold fast that which is good.

[22] Abstain from all appearance of evil.

[23] And the very God of peace sanctify you wholly; and I pray God your whole spirit and soul and body be preserved blameless unto the coming of our Lord Jesus Christ.

[24] Faithful is he that calleth you, who also will do it. [1 Thessalonians 5:5:24]

Less than a decade later, in the years of our Lord 60-62 A.D., the apostle Paul reveals the Whole Armour of God in his epistle to the Asian churches, amongst which was the foremost of the Christian churches in Ephesus. The epistle informed new congregations of their spiritual blessings, and the favour God bestowed on all followers of His Son. It also describes the battlefield upon which the forces of good and evil dwell, and the armaments they possess. The Whole Armour of God, described by Paul in Ephesians 6:10-20, was provided so that we might stand against the wiles of the devil. And in this light, it is appropriate to consider the opposing battlefield leaders, namely God and the devil. The devil is powerful, but he is not all powerful. He can only do what God allows him to do, and this is particularly noteworthy when it comes to Christians.[77] Only God is all powerful, or *"omnipotent,"*[78] as Holy Scripture states. And God is everywhere, as He is omnipresent. The devil is limited to where he can be and what he can do. Satan roams the earth;[79] therefore, he cannot be in more than one place at a time. God indwells every Christian,[80] at the same time, no matter where they are. And our Lord God is omniscient, in that He knows all things, with absolute understanding and awareness. Knowing Holy Scripture reveals these truths, and the means by which we effectively avoid and combat evil and live a godly life. The truth is: Satan is a defeated foe!

Know God:
This Comes From Reading the Holy Bible

"Finally, my brethren, be strong in the Lord,
and in the power of his might.
Put on the whole armour of God,
that ye may be able to stand against the wiles of the devil."
~~~ Ephesians 6:10-11

Know the Enemies of God:
The Devil, the World, and the Flesh.

"For we wrestle not against flesh and blood,
but against principalities, against powers,
against the rulers of the darkness of this world,
against spiritual wickedness in high places."
~~~ Ephesians 6:12

---

[77] Psalm 29:11; Psalm 119:165.
[78] Revelation 19:6.
[79] Job 1:7
[80] Matthew 18:20; John 14:15-17, 23; Hebrews 13:5; 1 John 4:16.

Fight the Good Fight:
Obey God and Leave All the Consequences to Him

"Wherefore take unto you the whole armour of God,
that ye may be able to withstand in the evil day,
and having done all, to stand."
~~~ Ephesians 6:13

Know the Truth of God:
Father, Son, & Holy Spirit
(Salvation comes only through His Son, Christ Jesus)

"Stand therefore, having your loins girt about with truth,
and having on the breastplate of righteousness;"
~~~ Ephesians 6:14

Walk in the Knowledge of the Gospel

"And your feet shod with the preparation of the gospel of peace;"
~~~ Ephesians 6:15

Live by Faith:
Believe God's Word is Absolute Truth

"Above all, taking the shield of faith, wherewith ye shall be able to
quench all the fiery darts of the wicked."
~~~ Ephesians 6:16

Salvation Rests in Christ Alone & Knowing Holy Scripture Counters
Spiritual Deception & Accusations
(Jesus said this & taught this when encountered by satan in the wilderness)

"And take the helmet of salvation, and the sword of the Spirit,
which is the word of God:"
~~~ Ephesians 6:17

Prayer is Powerful:
Pray for Yourself and Others,
making specific requests to be in the will of God

"Praying always with all prayer and supplication in the Spirit,
and watching thereunto with all perseverance
and supplication for all saints;"
~~~ Ephesians 6:18

"And for me, that utterance may be given unto me,
that I may open my mouth boldly,
to make known the mystery of the gospel,
For which I am an ambassador in bonds:
that therein I may speak boldly, as I ought to speak."
~~~ Ephesians 6:19-20

Therefore, my brothers and sisters in Christ, put on the Whole Armour of God!

~~~~~~~~~~

"Finally, my brethren, be strong in the Lord, and in the power of his might.
Put on the whole armour of God,
that ye may be able to stand against the wiles of the devil."
~~~ Ephesians 6:10-11

Chapter 11
Making Friends

~ ~ ~ ~ ~

"A man that hath friends must shew himself friendly:
and there is a friend that sticketh closer than a brother."
~~~ Proverbs 18:24

"Henceforth I call you not servants;
for the servant knoweth not what his lord doeth:
but I have called you friends;
for all things that I have heard of my Father I have made known unto you."
~~~ John 15:15

"Iron sharpeneth iron; so a man sharpeneth the countenance of his friend."
~~~ Proverbs 27:17

"Finally, be ye all of one mind, having compassion one of another, love as
brethren, be pitiful, be courteous: Not rendering evil for evil, or railing for railing:
but contrariwise blessing; knowing that ye are thereunto called,
that ye should inherit a blessing."
~~~ 1 Peter 3:8-9

~ ~ ~ ~ ~

Making friends is often called a difficult thing to do in our daily walk. But the truth of the matter is: if you want to make friends, then you need to be friendly.[81]

Time and again, we see simple and direct instructions contained in Holy Scripture for achieving success, whether it be making friends or living a godly life. Friends smile and are welcoming. They dwell on good things about one another. They

---

[81] Proverbs 18:24.

speak the truth and share intimate things. Friends do not return anger for anger. They understand not everyone has a great day every day. We are prone to having moods, both positive and negative. Grouchiness, for lack of a better word, happens, even amongst the best of friends. Holy Scripture says to show yourself *"friendly"*[82] if you want friends. It does not say, *"Be friendly only when others are friendly to you!"* We are to be *"friendly"*[83] even when others are unfriendly toward us. Friends develop bonds that transcend all other acquaintances.

Friends have duties to one another. They think the best of one another, and they desire good for one another. When times are tough, friends share burdens and pray for one another. It is during times like these that friends notice the facial expressions and feelings of those whom they have befriended. Holy Scripture calls this observing the *"countenance"*[84] of a friend. And it is something observed by God. We read about His first such observation in the Book of Genesis in regard to Cain,[85] and thereafter observations of countenance are mentioned repeatedly throughout the Word of God.[86] We are bound by Holy Scripture to help sharpen and lift the countenance of friends. This is what is meant in Proverbs 27:17 when we read, *"Iron sharpeneth iron; so a man sharpeneth the countenance of his friend."* This is an act of edification we are called to do.

---

[82] Proverbs 18:24.

[83] Ibid.

[84] Proverbs 27:17.

[85] Genesis 4:5-6: *"But unto Cain and to his offering he had not respect. And Cain was very wroth, and his countenance fell. And the Lord said unto Cain, Why art thou wroth? and why is thy countenance fallen?"*

[86] Genesis 4:5-6; 1 Samuel 1:18; 1 Samuel 16:12; 1 Samuel 17:42; 1 Samuel 25:3; 2 Samuel 14:27; Songs 2:14; Daniel 1:15; Daniel 5:6, 9, 10; Daniel 7:28; Daniel 8:23; Proverbs 15:13, 23; Proverbs 27:17; 2 Kings 8:11; Ezekiel 27:35; Nehemiah 2:2, 3; Ecclesiastes 7:3; Job 14:20; Job 29:24; Psalm 4:6; Psalm 10:4; Psalm 41:11; Psalm 42:5; Psalm 43:5; Psalm 44:3; Psalm 80:16; Psalm 89:15; Psalm 90:8; Luke 9:29.

Of course, the way to lose a friend is to violate those bonds and duties. Not supporting your friendship, sharing confidences that were meant only for you as a friend, or by lying, or perhaps doing anything that would identify you as being unfriendly, would be cause for losing a friend. And, in that light, consider your character and reputation. Is what you do consistent with a follower of Christ? If you are known as someone who is unfriendly in word or deed, or your bad works, chances are you will not find friends worth having. It is always best to build upon your personal relationship with Christ, and conform to His image. You will never be alone!

Understand, people make mistakes, but the key to success is learning from them. And it is here we demonstrate the quality and virtue of mercy and forgiveness. Friends show mercy and forgiveness to friends. I have always found it more desirable to keep friends and learn from mistakes, preferably the mistakes of others, as opposed to making those mistakes myself. And in this regard, understand good friends forgive and show mercy, and bear the fruit of the Spirit, which includes *"love, joy, peace, patience, kindness, goodness, faithfulness, gentleness, [and] self-control"* [*Galatians 5:22-23, NASB*]. These are the outward signs that God dwells in us.

But the awesome revelation of this chapter is not how to make friends. Rather, it is the knowledge that *"there is a friend that sticketh closer than a brother."*[87] This is an express reference to the Lord Jesus Christ. It is an absolute statement on those who accept Jesus Christ as their Lord and Saviour.

As Christ Jesus states in John 15:15, *"Henceforth I call you not servants; for the servant knoweth not what his lord doeth: but I have called you friends; for all things that I have heard of my Father I have made known unto you."* The unfortunate truth of this verse

---

[87] Proverbs 18:24.

is: Unsaved people know nothing of the friendship of Christ. God still loves them, but they are lost in their sin. They live a profoundly sad existence.

We who follow the Lord Jesus Christ are blessed beyond measure! We might err and fall short, perhaps even turn our back on God in our most trying times, but He has promised in Hebrews 13:5, *"I will never leave thee, nor forsake thee."* This is an absolute and unconditional friend. *"A friend,"* as Holy Scripture tells us, *"that sticketh closer than a brother."*[88] This is the central meaning of the new covenant,[89] not God visiting or walking with His people as was the case in the Old Testament,[90] but God abiding in His people, as we read in the New Testament.[91] This was the mission of Christ Jesus, that is, to restore our personal relationship with God. And He did that for you!

~~~~~~~~~~~

"A man that hath friends must shew himself friendly:
and there is a friend that sticketh closer than a brother."
~~~ *Proverbs 18:24*

---

[88] Proverbs 18:24.

[89] Matthew 26:28, NKJV: *"For this is My blood of the new covenant, which is shed for many for the remission of sins."*; Matthew 26:28; Mark 14:24; Luke 22:20.

[90] Genesis 5:22, 24; Genesis 6:9; Psalm 55:14.

[91] Matthew 18:20; John 14:15-17, 23; Hebrews 13:5; 1 John 4:16.

Chapter 12
What God Hath Joined

~ ~ ~ ~ ~

"And the LORD God said, It is not good that the man should be alone;
I will make him an help meet for him.
Therefore shall a man leave his father and his mother,
and shall cleave unto his wife: and they shall be one flesh."
~~~ Genesis 2:18, 24

"Whoso findeth a wife findeth a good thing, and obtaineth favour of the Lord."
~~~ Proverbs 18:22

"Likewise, ye wives, be in subjection to your own husbands;
that, if any obey not the word, they also may without the word be won by the
conversation of the wives; While they behold your chaste conversation coupled
with fear. Whose adorning let it not be that outward adorning of plaiting the hair,
and of wearing of gold, or of putting on of apparel; But let it be the hidden man of
the heart, in that which is not corruptible, even the ornament of a meek and quiet
spirit, which is in the sight of God of great price. For after this manner in the old
time the holy women also, who trusted in God, adorned themselves, being in
subjection unto their own husbands: Even as Sara obeyed Abraham, calling him
lord: whose daughters ye are, as long as ye do well,
and are not afraid with any amazement.

Likewise, ye husbands, dwell with them according to knowledge, giving honour
unto the wife, as unto the weaker vessel, and as being heirs together of the grace
of life; that your prayers be not hindered.

Finally, be ye all of one mind, having compassion one of another, love as brethren,
be pitiful, be courteous: Not rendering evil for evil, or railing for railing:
but contrariwise blessing; knowing that ye are thereunto called,
that ye should inherit a blessing."
~~~ 1 Peter 3:1-9

~ ~ ~ ~ ~

Marriage is sacred! This is something that must be

fundamentally understood in any discussion of the subject. It is, according to Holy Scripture, creations of God[92] that *"God hath joined together."[93]* The union of one man with one woman, by and with Almighty God. It is one of the profoundest creations of God at the foundation of the world. And it was at that time, following the creation of man, in Genesis 2:18, we learn, *"And the LORD God said, It is not good that the man should be alone; I will make him an help meet for him."* This brought forth God's creation of the woman and wife, and God shared the model of this covenant when He said in Genesis 2:24, *"Therefore shall a man leave his father and his mother, and shall cleave unto his wife: and they shall be one flesh."* One man, one woman, united together with God. This is the Covenant of Marriage.

So there is no doubt, God considers Marriage important. So much so, that Marriage is spoken of throughout the Old Testament,[94] as well as the New.[95] Jesus even began His many miracles at a marriage in Cana of Galilee,[96] where He turned water into wine, and as Holy Scripture tells us, He *"manifested forth his glory; and his disciples believed on Him."[97]* And Jesus himself spoke of Marriage as an unbreakable covenant when He said in Mark 10:9, *"What therefore God hath joined together, let not man put asunder."* If Marriage is that important to God, then it should be important to us!

And it deserves noting that marriage brings forth blessings. It is a cure for loneliness,[98] help in time of need,[99] a source of

---

[92] Genesis 2:7, 22.

[93] Mark 10:9.

[94] Genesis 34:9; Exodus 21:10; Deuteronomy 7:3; Joshua 23:12; Psalm 78:63.

[95] Matthew 22:2; Matthew 22:4; Matthew 22:9; Matthew 22:30; Matthew 24:38; Matthew 25:10; Mark 12:25; Luke 17:27; Luke 20:34; Luke 20:35; John 2:1; John 2:2; 1 Corinthians 7:38; Hebrews 13:4; Revelation 19:7; Revelation 19:9.

[96] John 2:1-11.

[97] John 2:11.

[98] Genesis 2:18.

[99] Ibid.

exhortation,[100] and the discovery of a best friend. And Proverbs 18:22 tells us, *"Whoso findeth a wife findeth a good thing, and obtaineth favour of the Lord."* Marriage is a great blessing!

Remember this: Marriage is miraculous! Holy Scripture tells us a married couple is *"one flesh."*[101] This is a creation of God. Positive and frequent communications are key to building upon this godly relationship. And if you are married, this communication is with God and your spouse. And on this point, I make the following two comments.

(1) Your spouse is supposed to be your best friend, next to the Lord. Treat them with respect and deference. When a spouse disagrees with you, do not react as if you are under attack. Do not render evil. Take it as a constructive opinion. It may be a valid opinion, or it may not. The point is to listen with kindness and gentleness, as these are fruit of the Spirit, knowing that all comments made to you are coming from a person who loves you and has your best interests at heart. This is being godly and giving a blessing to your best friend.

(2) In this book, I strongly encourage prayer. God commands it![102] So pray! Pray that your words to your spouse are edifying and pleasing to God. Ask God to make you the person He desires you to be in your marriage. Demonstrate faith, hope and love. Share these prayers and desires of your heart with your spouse. Let your spouse know of your ongoing commitment to do the will of God, which is to be joyful in marriage and to be the

---

[100] Hebrews 10:25.
[101] Genesis 2:24; Mark 10:8.
[102] 1 Thessalonians 5:17.

person and spouse conformed to the image of Christ. Communicate together in prayer to God. It is an amazing experience!

With all of this said, I have also heard friends happily married lament certain passages of Scripture, such as Mark 12:25 *["For when they shall rise from the dead, they neither marry, nor are given in marriage; but are as the angels which are in heaven."]* and Matthew 22:30 *["For in the resurrection they neither marry, nor are given in marriage, but are as the angels of God in heaven."]* The implication here is that marriages will no longer exist in the second coming or in heaven, and we might somehow lose our best friend.

In this perceived dilemma, we need to realize the Gospel is always Good News to the believer. I say this because we need to view these passages in context. Matthew 22:30 simply states that *"in the resurrection they neither marry, nor are given in marriage."* That literally means there will be no more marriages in the afterlife. There is no mention of us losing our spouses in heaven, or a breaking of the marriage covenant once we die. Scripture says we will be *"as the angels"*[103] of God in heaven. And 1 John 3:2 provides us the great hope and reassurance that we will be even closer to our spouses in heaven, *"Beloved, now are we the sons of God, and it doth not yet appear what we shall be: but we know that, when He shall appear, we shall be like Him; for we shall see Him as He is."* Note, *"we shall be like Him,"*[104] which means having greater love than we could ever have as human beings. We will have His unconditional, irrevocable love, and that love will be for our Lord as well as our spouse. No union could be greater! It is a powerful testimony!

---

[103] Mark 12:25 & Matthew 22:30.
[104] 1 John 3:2.

However, despite the magnificent beauty of the marriage covenant, we find in legal parlance that marriage is nothing more than a mere *"contract."* A contract is a legal instrument whereby one person makes an *"offer,"* another *"accepts"* the offer, and *"consideration"* is made. And being a contract, it can be broken, breached, modified, or enforced, depending upon a person's feelings or desires at the movement. Contracts can be made between any adults and/or businesses, provided they have the capacity to enter into one, and it is not made under duress. But there is a bright line distinction between contracts and biblical covenants. Contracts are man-made, but biblical covenants are made by God, and in this respect marriages are unique and very special.

Ending marriages in divorce, breaking covenants with God because of occasional feelings and seasons of discontent, forsaking your spouse for another, adultery, redefining marriage because it is popular to do so or politically in fashion, are never the way to go. They are abominations! And Leviticus 18:22-30 foretells the consequences of such abominations to the offender and their nation:

> [22] Thou shalt not lie with mankind, as with womankind: it is abomination.
>
> [23] Neither shalt thou lie with any beast to defile thyself therewith: neither shall any woman stand before a beast to lie down thereto: it is confusion.
>
> [24] Defile not ye yourselves in any of these things: for in all these the nations are defiled which I cast out before you:
>
> [25] And the land is defiled: therefore I do visit the iniquity thereof upon it, and the land itself vomiteth out her inhabitants.

^{26} Ye shall therefore keep my statutes and my judgments, and shall not commit any of these abominations; neither any of your own nation, nor any stranger that sojourneth among you:

^{27} (For all these abominations have the men of the land done, which were before you, and the land is defiled;)

^{28} That the land spue not you out also, when ye defile it, as it spued out the nations that were before you.

^{29} For whosoever shall commit any of these abominations, even the souls that commit them shall be cut off from among their people.

^{30} Therefore shall ye keep mine ordinance, that ye commit not any one of these abominable customs, which were committed before you, and that ye defile not yourselves therein: I am the LORD your God.

Furthermore, Isaiah 5:20 cautions, *"Woe unto them that call evil good, and good evil; that put darkness for light, and light for darkness; that put bitter for sweet, and sweet for bitter!"* These practices are not consistent with the Word of God, and because they are not, we learn of the consequences of such behavior in Romans 1:18-32:

^{18} For the wrath of God is revealed from heaven against all ungodliness and unrighteousness of men, who hold the truth in unrighteousness;

^{19} Because that which may be known of God is manifest in them; for God hath shewed it unto them.

[20] For the invisible things of him from the creation of the world are clearly seen, being understood by the things that are made, even his eternal power and Godhead; so that they are without excuse:

[21] Because that, when they knew God, they glorified him not as God, neither were thankful; but became vain in their imaginations, and their foolish heart was darkened.

[22] Professing themselves to be wise, they became fools,

[23] And changed the glory of the uncorruptible God into an image made like to corruptible man, and to birds, and fourfooted beasts, and creeping things.

[24] Wherefore God also gave them up to uncleanness through the lusts of their own hearts, to dishonour their own bodies between themselves:

[25] Who changed the truth of God into a lie, and worshipped and served the creature more than the Creator, who is blessed for ever. Amen.

[26] For this cause God gave them up unto vile affections: for even their women did change the natural use into that which is against nature:

[27] And likewise also the men, leaving the natural use of the woman, burned in their lust one toward another; men with men working that which is unseemly, and receiving in themselves that recompence of their error which was meet.

²⁸ And even as they did not like to retain God in their knowledge, God gave them over to a reprobate mind, to do those things which are not convenient;

²⁹ Being filled with all unrighteousness, fornication, wickedness, covetousness, maliciousness; full of envy, murder, debate, deceit, malignity; whisperers,

³⁰ Backbiters, haters of God, despiteful, proud, boasters, inventors of evil things, disobedient to parents,

³¹ Without understanding, covenantbreakers, without natural affection, implacable, unmerciful:

³² Who knowing the judgment of God, that they which commit such things are worthy of death, not only do the same, but have pleasure in them that do them.

These are the stark consequences of disobedience. It is what happens when we ignore the Word of God and call something evil *"good,"* and something good *"evil."* Breaking covenants is never the way to success or positive personal growth. The Bible is replete with such examples. Doesn't it make sense to obey God, reap the blessings, and leave the consequences to Him?

In my own walk, I have heard many rationalize their behavior. They argue from personal desire, not seeing things as God sees them. They see things from their own eyes. We hear, *"well, even Jesus said divorce is permitted."* Did He? They often cite Matthew 19:9 out of context, when Jesus said, *"Whosoever shall put away his wife, except it be for fornication, and shall marry another, committeth adultery: and whoso marrieth her which is put away doth commit adultery."* People narrowly interpret this to mean divorce is permitted when one spouse is engaged in an adulterous relationship, but they are wrong. Jesus was citing a precept of Moses because of the harness of peoples' hearts. People who rationalize divorce fail to cite the previous verse, Matthew 19:8, where Jesus said unto them, *"Moses because of the hardness of your hearts suffered you to put away your wives: but from the beginning it was not so."* And in this same conversation with the Pharisees in Mark 10:5, Jesus said of Moses, *"For the hardness of your heart he wrote you this precept."* Jesus was talking about how the hardness of hearts turned men from the Word of God, and how divorce was a *"precept"* of man, not a commandment of God. It is particularly noteworthy that Jesus said, *"but from the beginning it was not so."*[105] Remember, if it was not so with God from the beginning, it was not so with God then, now, or in the future. God is the same yesterday, today, and tomorrow. As we just read from Romans 1:28, *"God gave them over to a reprobate mind, to do those things which are not convenient."* Divorce from the time of Moses was rebellion against God's plan of marriage. *"God also gave them up to uncleanness through the lusts of their own hearts, to dishonour their own bodies between themselves: Who changed the truth of God into a lie,"* states Romans 1:24-25. Changing the truth of God to fit our personal desires is changing the truth of God into a lie. Do not follow your own desires, follow God's desires! Proverbs 3:5-6 states, *"⁵Trust in the Lord with all thine heart; and lean not unto thine own understanding. ⁶In all thy ways acknowledge him, and he shall direct thy paths."*

Know this truth: In Matthew 19, Jesus was affirming the covenant of marriage, as God established it in Genesis 2:24: *"Therefore shall a man leave his father and his mother, and shall cleave unto his wife: and they shall be one flesh."* And we know with absolute certainty that Jesus was affirming this life-long covenant because He said so Himself in Matthew 19:4-6, when He responded to the Pharisees who tempted Him on interpreting the law. Jesus said, *"⁴Have ye not read, that he which made them at the beginning made them male and female, ⁵ And said, For this cause*

---

[105] Matthew 19:8.

shall a man leave father and mother, and shall cleave to his wife: and they twain shall be one flesh? [6] Wherefore they are no more twain, but one flesh. What therefore God hath joined together, let not man put asunder." This is Jesus stating and re-affirming Holy Scripture. The covenant of marriage is not to be broken by any man! One man, one woman, united together with God. This is the covenant of Marriage. Know this truth!

Furthermore, I have heard the argument, *"Divorce is allowable if either the husband or wife is unsaved."* This is not Scriptural! Those who argue such cite 2 Corinthians 6:14: *"Be ye not unequally yoked together with unbelievers: for what fellowship hath righteousness with unrighteousness? and what communion hath light with darkness?"*

However, they again take Holy Scripture out of context. They link the casual associations of believers with the covenant of marriage. This is error. This is changing the truth of God to fit our personal desires. This is changing, as Romans 1:25 states, *"the truth of God into a lie."* The Word of God speaks directly to this situation of a marriage involving a believer and a non-believer. In 1 Corinthians 7:10-14, we read of this and God's *"command"* to married couples:

> [10] And unto the married I command, yet not I, but the Lord, Let not the wife depart from her husband:
>
> [11] But and if she depart, let her remain unmarried or be reconciled to her husband: and let not the husband put away his wife.
>
> [12] But to the rest speak I, not the Lord: If any brother hath a wife that believeth not, and she be pleased to dwell with him, let him not put her away.

¹³ And the woman which hath an husband that believeth not, and if he be pleased to dwell with her, let her not leave him.

¹⁴ For the unbelieving husband is sanctified by the wife, and the unbelieving wife is sanctified by the husband: else were your children unclean; but now are they holy.

Marriages are established by God. And make no mistake, if it pleases God, it can be for the evangelization of the spouse, and this would be to the glory of God. Think about it! This is a powerful testament! *"The unbelieving husband is sanctified by the [believing] wife, and the unbelieving wife is sanctified by the [believing] husband."*[106] And as a result of this union, God assures us, *"else were your children unclean; but now are they holy."*[107] This is a blessing from God for those who abide by His Word.

Remember, you were called by God for the purpose of *"giving a blessing,"*[108] so *"that you might inherit a blessing."*[109] This applies to you, and if you are married, to applies to your relationship with your spouse. Honor this covenant, the sacred oath you took to God and your spouse, and believe in the power of God! Know it, use it, and share it! You will be a blessing to your spouse, to others, and your nation. 2 Chronicles 7:14 assures of this promise of God, *"If my people, which are called by my name, shall humble themselves, and pray, and seek my face, and turn from their wicked ways; then will I hear from heaven, and will forgive their sin, and will heal their land."* Count on it!

---

[106] 1 Corinthians 7:14.
[107] Ibid.
[108] 1 Peter 3:9.
[109] Ibid.

It is a simple principle of Scripture: Obey God and leave all the consequences to Him. I never heard this truth so simply stated, until I heard it from a godly man.[110] It was one of his life learning principles, gleamed from his 80-plus years of life, and a walk with God just shy of that. Yet, it is difficult for men, even impossible, to obey God. It is a matter of Faith that we obey, and, as Romans 10:17 states, *"So then faith cometh by hearing, and hearing by the Word of God."* Faith comes from God, and He speaks to us primarily through His Word, and through godly counsel from other believers based on Scripture, and through our circumstances. And this makes all the more sense when we examine the words of Jesus, when He spoke about faith in Matthew 19:26, *"With men this is impossible; but with God all things are possible."*

The ultimate truth is that without God, there is no godly living, and no lasting personal growth or success. It is the road that leads to destruction. So the only way to a godly life is through God. With Him, we have all of our needs met, marriages endure and grow, and we have an immovable, unchanging foundation when all about us stumbles and falls. And He has promised to never leave of forsake us.[111] This is blessed assurance! A great Hope! *"Now faith is the substance of things hoped for,"* we read in Hebrews 11:1, *"the evidence of things not seen."* And as a dear friend of mine, Vickie Hafer,[112] shared godly counsel with me in my greatest valley experience, *"Hope in the promises of God is the foundation of our Faith ... always Hope!"* How right she was ... and is! Proverbs 13:12 says, *"Hope deferred maketh the heart sick: but when the desire cometh, it is a tree of life."* So Hope! *"Be of good courage,"* says the psalmist in Psalm 31:24, *"and he shall strengthen your heart, all*

---

[110] Dr. Charles F. Stanley, Senior Pastor, First Baptist Church of Atlanta.

[111] Hebrews 13:5.

[112] Vickie Hafer, Vice President & Ministries Director, Air Minister, The Lighthouse WECC 89.3 FM, St. Marys, GA.

ye that hope in the Lord." Hope[113] is essential to godly living!

~~~~~~~~~~

"If my people, which are called by my name, shall humble themselves,
and pray, and seek my face, and turn from their wicked ways;
then will I hear from heaven, and will forgive their sin, and will heal their land."
~~~ 2 Chronicles 7:14

---

[113] Psalm 16:9; Psalm 22:9; Psalm 21:3; Psalm 31:24; Psalm 33:18; Psalm 33:22; Psalm 38:15; Psalm 39:7; Psalm 42:5; Psalm 42:11; Psalm 43:5; Psalm 71:5; Psalm 71:14; Psalm 78:7; Psalm 119:43; Psalm 119:49; Psalm 119:74; Psalm 119:81; Psalm 119:114; Psalm 119:116; Psalm 119:147; Psalm 119:166; Psalm 130:5; Psalm 130:7; Psalm 131:3; Psalm 146:5; Psalm 147:11; Proverbs 10:28; Proverbs 13:12; Proverbs 14:32; Proverbs 19:18; Ecclesiastes 9:4; Jeremiah 14:8; Jeremiah 17:7; Jeremiah 17:13; Jeremiah 17:17; Jeremiah 31:17; Jeremiah 50:7; Lamentations 3:18; Lamentations 3:21; Lamentations 3:24; Lamentations 3:26; Lamentations 3:29; Ezekiel 13:6; Hosea 2:15; Joel 3:16; Zechariah 9:12; Acts 2:26; Acts 23:6; Acts 24:15; Acts 26:6; Acts 26:7; Romans 4:18; Romans 5:2; Romans 5:4; Romans 5:5; Romans 8:20; Romans 8:24; Romans 8:25; Romans 12:12; Romans 15:4; Romans 15:13; 1 Corinthians 9:10; 1 Corinthians 13:7; 1 Corinthians 13:13; 1 Corinthians 15:19; 2 Corinthians 3:12; 2 Corinthians 10:15; Galatians 5:5; Ephesians 1:18; Ephesians 4:4; Philippians 1:20; Colossians 1:5; Colossians 1:23; Colossians 1:27; 1 Thessalonians 1:13; 1 Thessalonians 2:19; 1 Thessalonians 5:8; 2 Thessalonians 2:16; 1 Timothy 1:1; Titus 1:2; Titus 2:13; Titus 3:7; Hebrews 3:6; Hebrews 6:11; Hebrews 6:18; Hebrews 6:19; Hebrews 7:19; Hebrews 11:1; 1 Peter 1:3; 1 Peter 1:13; 1 Peter 1:21; 1 Peter 3:15; 1 John 3:3.

Chapter 13
Woe unto You ... Lawyers!

~ ~ ~ ~ ~

"What therefore God hath joined together, let not man put asunder."
~~~ Mark 10:9

"Then answered one of the lawyers, and said unto him,
Master, thus saying thou reproachest us also.
And he said, Woe unto you also, ye lawyers! for ye lade men with burdens
grievous to be borne, and ye yourselves touch not the burdens
with one of your fingers.
Woe unto you! for ye build the sepulchres of the prophets,
and your fathers killed them.
Truly ye bear witness that ye allow the deeds of your fathers:
for they indeed killed them, and ye build their sepulchres."
~~~ Luke 11:45-48

"Woe unto them that call evil good, and good evil;
that put darkness for light, and light for darkness; that put bitter for sweet, and
sweet for bitter!"
~~~ Isaiah 5:20

~ ~ ~ ~ ~

It deserves noting that I am an attorney and counselor at law, but a follower of Christ first. So I can comment on the legal profession in a manner much like the Apostle Paul did on the disposition of the Jews at his revelation that he himself was a Christian and one schooled in the Mosaic Law, as he was also a Pharisee.

The truth is: We have in our legal systems in America and around the world a stark clash with the Word of God. I will explain what I mean, and I will do so from a position of knowledge and experience. In addition to being an attorney and counselor at Law, and a former county judge and a city chief judge, I was a professor of law at an American law school. I am quite familiar with the Law. But more importantly, I am familiar with the Word of God, and dedicated to a daily walk with the Lord, which includes reading and meditating on Holy Scripture each and every day. I hold fast to the proposition that Psalm 119:102 is true: *"Thy Word is a lamp unto my feet, and a light unto my path."*

In Mark 10:2-12, we read the following:

[2] And the Pharisees came to him, and asked him, Is it lawful for a man to put away his wife? tempting him.

[3] And he answered and said unto them, What did Moses command you?

[4] And they said, Moses suffered to write a bill of divorcement, and to put her away.

[5] And Jesus answered and said unto them, For the hardness of your heart he wrote you this precept.

[6] But from the beginning of the creation God made them male and female.

[7] For this cause shall a man leave his father and mother, and cleave to his wife;

[8] And they twain shall be one flesh: so then they are no more twain, but one flesh.

[9] What therefore God hath joined together, let not man put asunder.

[10] And in the house his disciples asked him again of the same matter.

[11] And he saith unto them, Whosoever shall put away his wife, and marry another, committeth adultery against her.

12 And if a woman shall put away her husband, and be married to another, she committeth adultery. [Mark 10:2-12]

God's admonishment is clear: *"What therefore God hath joined together, let not man put asunder."*[114] No man is allowed to break this Covenant, not the husband, not the wife, not the lawyer, and not the judge. *"Let not man,"*[115] is a clear admonition that no man is to interfere with or attempt to break this covenant of God!

As noted in the previous chapter concerning Matthew 19, the same is true and consistent with Mark 10, Jesus was talking about how the hardness of hearts turned men from the Word of God. As Romans 1:28 notes, *"God gave them over to a reprobate mind, to do those things which are not convenient."* Divorce from the time of Moses was rebellion against God's plan of marriage. The same is true today! As Roman 1:24-25 observes, *"God also gave them up to uncleanness through the lusts of their own hearts, to dishonour their own bodies between themselves: Who changed the truth of God into a lie."* Changing the truth of God to fit our personal desires, no matter who tells you it is alright to do so, be it a lawyer or judge, is changing the truth of God into a lie. Do not follow your own desires, follow God's desires! And listen to no man or woman who suggests a course of action that is in violation of Holy Scripture. Proverbs 3:5-6 states, *"⁵Trust in the Lord with all thine heart; and lean not unto thine own understanding. ⁶In all thy ways acknowledge him, and he shall direct thy paths."*

Yet, despite this truth, we see more than half of all marriages end in divorce. And we are hard-pressed not to see billboard signs on any major highway promoting divorce by some lawyer. In fact, those kinds of advertisements are just about everywhere: on television, radio, the internet, you name it! Even in my home state

---

[114] Mark 10:9.
[115] Ibid.

of Georgia, we have something called *"no fault divorce."* It reminds me of *"no fault insurance."* We have so trivialized the sacred covenant of marriage that to end it is easier and often less expensive than coach airfare from one city to another. And, by the way, divorce is often promoted as a *"Special,"* meaning you can get one cheaper during limited *"sale"* times. It is disgusting and, more importantly, contrary to the Word of God!

And it is not only the so-called *"family law"* lawyers promoting divorces who are at fault. It is the judges who casually grant divorce orders, and the legislatures who have enacted so-called *"no fault divorce"* laws that are to blame as well. This is no doubt *"heresy"* to most in today's legal profession, and I cannot help but think how tall the legal profession stood mere decades ago. That was a time when lawyers in America could be disbarred for advertising. And it was a time many lawyers understood and professed that our modern civil and criminal codes were based on the laws of God. How far, or perhaps how low, we have gone since those golden days! Lest I digress.

Hollywood and the world have trivialized divorce, even encouraged it, as has the modern legal profession. And even in present day America, we find individual states have by judicial fiat redefined *"Marriage"* from being between one man and one woman, to same-sex couples. And they have established this in their state laws. This is an ominous precedent, as it now raises the legal question of whether neighboring states, or all states for that matter, must now honor that so-called newly established *"right"* within their own borders. I say this because such adaptations are part of the Full Fair and Credit Clause in the U.S. Constitution, which is found in Article IV, Section 1, and addresses the duties that states within the union have to respect the *"public acts, records, and judicial proceedings of every other state."* It is the reason we can have a driver's license in Georgia and drive to California, without having to have a driver's license from California or any of the states one would be traveling through to get there. The license of one state is honored by all others. It is also the reason we do not have to re-marry a spouse if we are originally married in New York and relocate in Florida. The marriage license of New York is honored and valid in the state of Florida, and vice versa. Allowing same-sex marriages in some states and not others creates a constitutional dilemma. And although we have the Defense of Marriage Act (DOMA),[116] which is a United States federal law passed by large majorities in the Congress and signed into law on September 21, 1996, the Obama Administration announced it would not enforce this law, although all in the administration, including the president, took an oath to uphold the Law. Under this DOMA Law, Marriage is defined as the legal union of one man and one woman for federal and inter-state recognition purposes in the United States, *and no U.S. state or political subdivision is required to recognize a same-sex marriage from another state.*[117]   But alas, even this is under challenge.

No doubt about it, Marriage is under attack, not only in the political arena, but in the spiritual realm as well. Even the National Cathedral in our nation's capital, which is arguably the most prominent of America's churches, having hosted presidents and mourned national tragedies, has opted to perform marriage ceremonies for gay, lesbian, bisexual, and transgender members.

Like it or not, the Word of God says in Leviticus 18:22, *"Thou shalt not lie with mankind, as with womankind: it is abomination."* This is the express Word of God. Believe it or not. The church would do well to believe!

But the real questions are: *What do I believe? And what should I do if I am having issues in my marriage?* The answers are: *Believe God! Seek God's answers through His Word. Seek godly counsel from believers, who can give godly advice. Seek out a pastor*

---

[116] Defense of Marriage Act (DOMA), Pub.L. 104-199, 110 Stat. 2419, enacted September 21, 1996, 1 U.S.C. § 7 and 28 U.S.C. § 1738C.
[117] Ibid.

or a priest, knowledgeable and trusting in the Word of God. Don't give up! And do not give into temptation! If you have to, contact me! This is the time to apply the admonition in 2 Corinthians 6:14: *"Be ye not unequally yoked together with unbelievers: for what fellowship hath righteousness with unrighteousness? and what communion hath light with darkness?"* Do not seek ungodly counsel! My strong recommendation is not to seek advice from a divorce attorney.

Trust and obey God, and leave all the consequences to Him! You will be blessed for it! And you will be a blessing to others!

~~~~~~~~~~

"What therefore God hath joined together, let not man put asunder."
~~~ Mark 10:9

Chapter 14
The Gathering of the Saints

~ ~ ~ ~ ~

"Not forsaking the assembling of ourselves together, as the manner of some is;
but exhorting one another: and so much the more,
as ye see the day approaching."
~~~ Hebrews 10:25

"For as the body is one, and hath many members,
and all the members of that one body, being many, are one body:
so also is Christ. For by one Spirit are we all baptized into one body,
whether we be Jews or Gentiles, whether we be bond or free; and have been all
made to drink into one Spirit. For the body is not one member, but many.
If the foot shall say, Because I am not the hand, I am not of the body; is it
therefore not of the body? And if the ear shall say, Because I am not the eye, I am
not of the body; is it therefore not of the body? If the whole body were an eye,
where were the hearing? If the whole were hearing, where were the smelling?
But now hath God set the members every one of them in the body,
as it hath pleased him. And if they were all one member, where were the body?
But now are they many members, yet but one body. And the eye cannot say unto
the hand, I have no need of thee: nor again the head to the feet, I have no need of
you. Nay, much more those members of the body, which seem to be more feeble,
are necessary: And those members of the body, which we think to be less
honourable, upon these we bestow more abundant honour; and our uncomely
parts have more abundant comeliness. For our comely parts have no need: but
God hath tempered the body together, having given more abundant honour to
that part which lacked. That there should be no schism in the body; but that the
members should have the same care one for another. And whether one member
suffer, all the members suffer with it; or one member be honoured, all the
members rejoice with it. Now ye are the body of Christ, and members in
particular. And God hath set some in the church, first apostles, secondarily
prophets, thirdly teachers, after that miracles, then gifts of healings, helps,
governments, diversities of tongues."
~~~ 1 Corinthians 12:12-28

~ ~ ~ ~ ~

We live in a fallen and dangerous world.   This is a sad truth, and by all reports it appears things are not getting better. Even in America, where the torch of liberty is supposed to burn brightest, we see a rapid falling away from the founding principles. Our highest Court has removed prayer and the 10 Commandments from our public schools. They divined a *"right"* in our Constitution of a *"woman's privacy,"* which legally sanctions the abortion of more than a million babies a year in America, while at the same time hypocritically decrying the death of a infinitesimally smaller number of children by evil men in school shootings. Are babies in the womb of less value than babies in elementary school? I pray not. The killing of any child is horrific. Children are a gift from God. And we see the sanctioning of same-sex marriage, despite the fact it is also contrary to the Word of God. We see evil called *"good,"* and good called *"narrow-minded"* and *"evil."* Isaiah 5:20 warns, *"Woe unto them that call evil good, and good evil; that put darkness for light, and light for darkness; that put bitter for sweet, and sweet for bitter!"*

But as bad as things are, they could be worse. Whenever I ponder the state of affairs in America or around the world, I think back to the story of Sodom and Gomorrah in Genesis. Abraham was troubled by the knowledge that God's judgment was at hand for these cities, and asked, *"Wilt thou also destroy the righteous with the wicked?"*[118] And God considered Abraham's prayer and promised to spare His terrible, swift judgment from those cities if there could be found just ten righteous men there.[119] The sad truth is not even ten good men could be found. Those cities were so exceedingly wicked that God utterly destroyed them.[120]

It is my conviction God has kept His protective hand on America because righteous men and women can be found. Hopefully, you encounter these righteous men and women every

---

[118] Genesis 18:23.
[119] Genesis 18:32.
[120] Genesis 19: 24-25.

day in your walk. However, if you do not, may I respectfully suggest you find them at the nearest Bible-believing church to your home?

Holy Scripture admonishes us *"not to forsake the assembling of ourselves together,"*[121] that is, fellow-believers whom He calls *"saints"*[122] and *"righteous"*[123] and *"holy,"*[124] part of *"a royal priesthood."*[125] For we are the children of God,[126] cloaked in His righteousness through the substitutionary sacrifice of His Son, our Lord Jesus Christ. We are not to neglect the gathering of the saints!

---

[121] Hebrews 10:25.

[122] 1 Samuel 2:9; 2 Chronicles 6:41; Psalm 16:3; Psalm 30:4; Psalm 31:23; Psalm 34:9; Psalm 37:28; Psalm 50:5; Psalm 52:9; Psalm 85:8; Psalm 89:5, 7; Psalm 97:10; Psalm 116:15; Psalm 132:9, 16; Psalm 145:10; Psalm 148:14; Psalm 149:1, 5, 9; Daniel 7:18, 21, 22, 25, 27; Hosea 11:12; Zechariah 14:5; Matthew 27:52; Acts 9:13, 32, 41; Acts 26:10; Romans 1:7; Romans 8:27; Romans 12:13; Romans 15:25, 26, 31; Romans 16:2, 15; 1 Corinthians 1:2; I Corinthians 6:1, 2; 1 Corinthians 14:33; 1 Corinthians 16:1, 15; 2 Corinthians 1:1; 2 Corinthians 8:4; 2 Corinthians 9:1, 12; 2 Corinthians 13:13; Ephesians 1:1, 15, 18; Ephesians 2:19; Ephesians 3:8, 18; Ephesians 4:12; Ephesians 5:3; Ephesians6:18; Philippians 1:1; Philippians 4:22; Colossians 1:2, 4, 12, 26; 1 Thessalonians 3:13; 2 Thessalonians 1:10; 1 Timothy 5:10; Philemon 1:5, 7; Hebrews 6:10; Hebrew 13:24; Jude 1:3, 14; Revelation 5:8; Revelation 8:3, 4; Revelation 11:18; Revelation 13:7, 10; Revelation 14:12; Revelation 15:3; Revelation 16:6; Revelation 17:6; Revelation 18:24; Revelation 19:8; Revelation 20:9.

[123] Genesis 7:1; Genesis 18:23, 24, 25, 26, 28;Genesis 38:26; Exodus 23:8; Numbers 23:10; Deuteronomy 16:19; Deuteronomy 25:1; 1 Samuel 24:17; 2 Samuel 4:11; 1 Kings 2:32; 1 Kings 8:32; 2 Kings 10:9; 2 Chronicles 6:23; Job 9:15; Job 17:9; Job 22:19; Job 23:7; Job 34:5; Job 35:7; Job 36:7; Job 40:8; Psalm 1:5, 6; Psalm 5:12; Psalm 7:11; Psalm 11:3, 5, 7; Psalm 14:5; Psalm 19:9; Psalm 31:18; Psalm 32:11; Psalm 33:1; Psalm 34:15, 17, 19; Psalm 37:16, 17, 21, 25, 29, 30, 32, 39; Psalm 52:6; Psalm 55:22; Psalm 58:10, 11; Psalm 64:10; Psalm 68:3; Psalm 69:28; Psalm 72:7; Psalm 75:10; Psalm 92:12; Psalm 94:21; Psalm 97:11, 12; Psalm 107:42; Psalm 112:4, 6; Psalm 118:20; Psalm 125:3; Psalm 140:13; Psalm 146:8; Proverbs 2:7, 20; Proverbs 3:32; Proverbs 10:3, 11, 16, 21, 24, 25, 28, 30, 32; Proverbs 11:8, 10, 21, 23, 28, 30, 31; Proverbs 12:3, 5, 7, 10, 12; Proverbs 12:26; Proverbs 13:5, 9, 21, 25; Proverbs 14:9, 19, 32; Proverbs 15:6; et al.

[124] Exodus 22:31; Exodus 29:33; Leviticus 11:44, 45; Leviticus 19:2; Leviticus 20:7, 26; Leviticus 21:6, 8; Leviticus 27:14; Numbers 6:5, 8; Numbers 15:40; Numbers 16:3, 5, 7; Deuteronomy 7:6; Deuteronomy 14:12, 21; Deuteronomy 26:19; Deuteronomy 28:9; 2 Kings 4:9; et al.

[125] 1 Peter 2:9.

[126] Matthew 5:9; Luke 20:36; Romans 8:16; 1 John 3:10; 1 John 5:2.

With that said, let us also remember our future success and eternal life with God is not dependent on what church we belong to, or whether we even go to church. It is not dependent on what religion we belong to, or don't belong to for that matter. And it is not dependent on how many Christian friends we gather with. It is, however, entirely dependent on our personal relationship with God. The heart of the matter is this: Do you believe Jesus Christ is your Lord and Saviour? The truth is this: Unless you believe, nothing in these pages will matter in the long run. If you do not believe, Christ still loves you, and He cares for you, but you cannot claim a personal relationship with Him, and you cannot claim Him as a friend or Him your friend.[127] Nor can you claim His many promises for your personal growth and success, and eternal life with Him.

Being a *"believer"* means accepting Jesus Christ as your Lord and Saviour. And as such, Jesus says to us in John 15:14, *"Ye are my friends, if ye do whatsoever I command you."* Can you imagine that? The Creator of heaven and earth, and the entire universe, calls us *"friends!"* And we demonstrate our friendship with the Lord by following His commandments. One of those commandments is not to forsake the gathering of the saints.[128]

Gathering with fellow-believers in the Lord Jesus Christ serves several purposes, no purpose being greater than for the glory of God. We gather together to worship God, to edify one another with the gifts that God has bestowed on each believer, to lift the countenance of friends, to carry out the Great Commission with the support of a friend or friends, to learn the burdens and praises of our brothers and sisters in Christ, and pray for them, and to build and strengthen the body of Christ. *"For God is not the author of confusion,"* we read in 1 Corinthians 14:33, *"but of peace, as in all*

---

[127] John 15:14-15.
[128] Hebrews 10:25.

the churches of the saints." We gather with fellow-believers because the Lord Jesus Christ calls on us to do so! You are needed!

Make no mistake about it, the future of America is in the hands of this gathering of the saints! Never underestimate the power of prayer and the collective influence of a righteous people on a holy God. Friends, there is a reason God gives us insight into His holy nature throughout Scripture. *"If my people,"* says the Lord God in 2 Chronicles 7:14, *"which are called by my name, shall humble themselves, and pray, and seek my face, and turn from their wicked ways; then will I hear from heaven, and will forgive their sin, and will heal their land."* He hears and answers the prayers of His people individually and collectively when they gather and pray for His hand on their lives and the affairs of their nation.

Know the will of God! He has a plan and a purpose especially for you! He loves you unconditionally! And He delights in your prayers, and your desire to have a closer, more personal relationship with Him through His Son! Living your life with and for God, where all things are possible, is living life at its very best!

Do not neglect the gathering of the saints!

~~~~~~~~~~

"These things I have spoken unto you, that in me ye might have peace.
In the world ye shall have tribulation: but be of good cheer;
I have overcome the world."
~~~ John 16:33

Chapter 15
Sons of God

~ ~ ~ ~ ~

"For as many as are led by the Spirit of God, they are the sons of God."
~~~ Romans 8:14

"Do all things without murmurings and disputings:
That ye may be blameless and harmless, the sons of God,
without rebuke, in the midst of a crooked and perverse nation,
among whom ye shine as lights in the world;
Holding forth the word of life; that I may rejoice in the day of Christ,
that I have not run in vain, neither laboured in vain."
~~~ Philippians 2:14-16

~ ~ ~ ~ ~

To be a Christian is special! It is to be led by the Holy Spirit, walking in Truth, conforming to the image of Christ Jesus, and having an ongoing desire to do the will of God. 1 Peter 2:9-10 states, *"⁹But ye are a chosen generation, a royal priesthood, an holy nation, a peculiar people; that ye should shew forth the praises of him who hath called you out of darkness into his marvellous light; ¹⁰Which in time past were not a people, but are now the people of God: which had not obtained mercy, but now have obtained mercy."*

The Word of God identifies believers as *"the sons of God,"*[129] which has deep and profound meaning when we realize Jesus was the Son of God. We are part of what Holy Scripture calls *"a royal priesthood,"*[130] *"saints"*[131] and *"righteous"*[132] and *"holy."*[133] For we

---

[129] Romans 8:14; Philippians 2:14-16.
[130] 1 Peter 2:9.

are the children of God,[134] cloaked in His righteousness through the substitutionary sacrifice of His Son, our Lord Jesus Christ.

But we live in a world that seeks to diminish the power and impact of Christ, and deceive those who follow Him as Lord. I have even heard self-professed Christians say, *"I am just a poor sinner,"* or *"I'm only human, of course I still sin!"* But how can that be, especially if we know the Word of God?

We who believe on the Lord Christ Jesus are *"saved,"* there is no condemnation.[135] In Psalm 103:12, we read, *"As far as the east is from the west, so far hath he removed our transgressions from*

---

[131] 1 Samuel 2:9; 2 Chronicles 6:41; Psalm 16:3; Psalm 30:4; Psalm 31:23; Psalm 34:9; Psalm 37:28; Psalm 50:5; Psalm 52:9; Psalm 85:8; Psalm 89:5, 7; Psalm 97:10; Psalm 116:15; Psalm 132:9, 16; Psalm 145:10; Psalm 148:14; Psalm 149:1, 5, 9; Daniel 7:18, 21, 22, 25, 27; Hosea 11:12; Zechariah 14:5; Matthew 27:52; Acts 9:13, 32, 41; Acts 26:10; Romans 1:7; Romans 8:27; Romans 12:13; Romans 15:25, 26, 31; Romans 16:2, 15; 1 Corinthians 1:2; I Corinthians 6:1, 2; 1 Corinthians 14:33; 1 Corinthians 16:1, 15; 2 Corinthians 1:1; 2 Corinthians 8:4; 2 Corinthians 9:1, 12; 2 Corinthians 13:13; Ephesians 1:1, 15, 18; Ephesians 2:19; Ephesians 3:8, 18; Ephesians 4:12; Ephesians 5:3; Ephesians6:18; Philippians 1:1; Philippians 4:22; Colossians 1:2, 4, 12, 26; 1 Thessalonians 3:13; 2 Thessalonians 1:10; 1 Timothy 5:10; Philemon 1:5, 7; Hebrews 6:10; Hebrew 13:24; Jude 1:3, 14; Revelation 5:8; Revelation 8:3, 4; Revelation 11:18; Revelation 13:7, 10; Revelation 14:12; Revelation 15:3; Revelation 16:6; Revelation 17:6; Revelation 18:24; Revelation 19:8; Revelation 20:9.

[132] Genesis 7:1; Genesis 18:23, 24, 25, 26, 28;Genesis 38:26; Exodus 23:8; Numbers 23:10; Deuteronomy 16:19; Deuteronomy 25:1; 1 Samuel 24:17; 2 Samuel 4:11; 1 Kings 2:32; 1 Kings 8:32; 2 Kings 10:9; 2 Chronicles 6:23; Job 9:15; Job 17:9; Job 22:19; Job 23:7; Job 34:5; Job 35:7; Job 36:7; Job 40:8; Psalm 1:5, 6; Psalm 5:12; Psalm 7:11; Psalm 11:3, 5, 7; Psalm 14:5; Psalm 19:9; Psalm 31:18; Psalm 32:11; Psalm 33:1; Psalm 34:15, 17, 19; Psalm 37:16, 17, 21, 25, 29, 30, 32, 39; Psalm 52:6; Psalm 55:22; Psalm 58:10, 11; Psalm 64:10; Psalm 68:3; Psalm 69:28; Psalm 72:7; Psalm 75:10; Psalm 92:12; Psalm 94:21; Psalm 97:11, 12; Psalm 107:42; Psalm 112:4, 6; Psalm 118:20; Psalm 125:3; Psalm 140:13; Psalm 146:8; Proverbs 2:7, 20; Proverbs 3:32; Proverbs 10:3, 11, 16, 21, 24, 25, 28, 30, 32; Proverbs 11:8, 10, 21, 23, 28, 30, 31; Proverbs 12:3, 5, 7, 10, 12; Proverbs 12:26; Proverbs 13:5, 9, 21, 25; Proverbs 14:9, 19, 32; Proverbs 15:6; et al.

[133] Exodus 22:31; Exodus 29:33; Leviticus 11:44, 45; Leviticus 19:2; Leviticus 20:7, 26; Leviticus 21:6, 8; Leviticus 27:14; Numbers 6:5, 8; Numbers 15:40; Numbers 16:3, 5, 7; Deuteronomy 7:6; Deuteronomy 14:12, 21; Deuteronomy 26:19; Deuteronomy 28:9; 2 Kings 4:9; et al.

[134] Matthew 5:9; Luke 20:36; Romans 8:16; 1 John 3:10; 1 John 5:2.

[135] Romans 8:1, *"There is therefore **now no condemnation** to them which are in Christ Jesus, who walk **not** after the flesh, but after the Spirit."*

us." God shares His level of forgiveness in Hebrews 10:17-18, when He states, *"¹⁷And their sins and iniquities will I remember no more. ¹⁸Now where remission of these is, there is no more offering for sin."* Moreover, Romans 6:14 declares, *"For sin shall not have dominion over you: for ye are not under the law, but under grace."* Sin has no place in the life of a Christian, because we dwell in a state of grace. *"But now being made free from sin, and become servants to God, ye have your fruit unto holiness, and the end everlasting life,"* notes the Apostle Paul in Romans 6:22. And he continues in Romans 6:23, *"For the wages of sin is death; but the gift of God is eternal life through Jesus Christ our Lord."* And lest there be any doubt, 1 John 3:9 declares, *"Whosoever is born of God doth not commit sin; for his seed remaineth in him: and he cannot sin, because he is born of God."* This is why Jesus could heal and rescue those oppressed during His ministry on earth, and affirmatively tell them, *"Sin no more."*[136] He meant it!

Sin does not exist in a state of grace. Christians might transgress and drift from the will of God, but we do not sin. Sin separates us from God, and if we still sin, then we would become separated from God and lose our salvation every time we sin. But the truth is: You cannot lose our salvation! You are either saved or a sinner, under grace or under the law, a son of God or a son of perdition,[137] found by God or lost and destined for hell. Do not be distracted by false doctrine and the wiles of the devil. Know the Truth!

And if you are one of the few who believe you actually could lose your salvation, you are wrong, and you need to study Holy Scripture. Jesus clearly said, *"I will never leave thee, nor forsake thee."*[138] Note the following exchange in John 10:24-29:

---

[136] John 5:14, *"Afterward Jesus findeth him in the temple, and said unto him, Behold, thou art made whole: **sin no more**, lest a worse thing come unto thee.";* John 8:11, *"She said, No man, Lord. And Jesus said unto her, Neither do I condemn thee: go, and **sin no more**."*

[137] John 17:12; Philippians 1:28; 2 Thessalonians 2:3; 1 Timothy 6:9; Hebrews 10:39; 2 Peter 3:7; Revelation 17:8, 11.

[138] Hebrews 13:5.

> ²⁴ Then came the Jews round about him, and said unto him, How long dost thou make us to doubt? If thou be the Christ, tell us plainly.
>
> ²⁵ Jesus answered them, I told you, and ye believed not: the works that I do in my Father's name, they bear witness of me.
>
> ²⁶ But ye believe not, because ye are not of my sheep, as I said unto you.
>
> ²⁷ My sheep hear my voice, and I know them, and they follow me:
>
> ²⁸ And I give unto them eternal life; and they shall never perish, neither shall any man pluck them out of my hand.
>
> ²⁹ My Father, which gave them me, is greater than all; and no man is able to pluck them out of my Father's hand.

Note Jesus says of the saved, *"neither shall any man pluck them out of my hand"*[139] and *"no man is able to pluck them out of my Father's hand."*[140] This means: Once saved = Always saved! That is the promise of God! Count on it!

We live in an age that would promote hopelessness and condemnation. Live your life with faith, hope, and love!

We also live in a time when many claim they can *"save"* themselves by leading a relatively good life. *"After all,"* they claim, *"I didn't kill anybody!"* Salvation is, as Ephesians 2:9 tells us, *"Not of works, lest any man should boast."* While most did not kill anyone, they are ignorant of the righteousness of God, His laws, and His Word. Otherwise, they would understand that salvation is not a

---

[139] John 10:28.
[140] John 10:29.

work of man, lest any man boast,[141] but a gift from God,[142] received only by the saving grace of our Lord.[143]

Even when we read the express words of Jesus, some will change them to suit their agenda. This is false doctrine. For example, in John 15:16, Jesus states, *"Ye have not chosen me, but I have chosen you, and ordained you, that ye should go and bring forth fruit, and that your fruit should remain: that whatsoever ye shall ask of the Father in my name, he may give it you."* However, I have heard many say, *"I chose to accept Christ."* This is not so, for as we read in Romans 3:11, *"There is none that understandeth, there is none that seeketh after God."* No one seeks God on their own accord. It is the work of the Holy Spirit that draws men to the free gift of God.

And herein we find the mission of the sons of God. We are led by the Holy Spirit to shine as light upon a lost and dying world. Not to live in condemnation or doubt, but in faith and hope and love. We are to know Truth, and to conform to the image of our Saviour and Lord, and seek that which is lost. To echo the call of repentance to a lost and dying world, for the kingdom of God is at hand. We are to answer the call of the Great Commission, and do the will of God. This is the quest of the sons of God.

~~~~~~~~~~

"So shall my word be that goeth forth out of my mouth:
it shall not return unto me void, but it shall accomplish that which I please,
and it shall prosper in the thing whereto I sent it."
~~~ Isaiah 55:11

---

[141] Ephesians 2:9.
[142] Romans 5:15.
[143] Romans 5:17.

Chapter 16

Choose Life

~ ~ ~ ~ ~

"But whoso shall offend one of these little ones which believe in me,
it were better for him that a millstone were hanged about his neck,
and that he were drowned in the depth of the sea."
~~~ Matthew 18:6

"Thou shalt not kill."
~~~ Exodus 20:13

"Lo, children are an heritage of the LORD:
and the fruit of the womb is his reward."
~~~ Psalm 127:3

"Before I formed thee in the belly I knew thee;
and before thou camest forth out of the womb I sanctified thee,
and I ordained thee a prophet unto the nations."
~~~ Jeremiah 1:5

~ ~ ~ ~ ~

Perhaps the most divisive *"social issue"* of our time is the issue of abortion, that is, the killing of helpless babies. There is one side, which calls it *"choice,"* and *"a woman's right."* And then there are those who call it *"wrong"* and *"murder,"* that is, the intentional taking of a life of another human being with malice aforethought. In the law, *"malice"* is an evil mind, and the word *"aforethought"* connotes a thought out plan. In my opinion, abortion is murder.

Children are a gift of God. Something God cherishes, and warns against harming in His Word. They are created in His image, for His purpose. But as a society we have ignored the admonishments of God, and choose death for these little ones.   As

Jesus shares in Matthew 25:40, *"Verily I say unto you, Inasmuch as ye have done it unto one of the least of these my brethren, ye have done it unto me."*

Believe me, I understand the arguments, and I will not belabor the points or sugarcoat them. Abortion is inconsistent with the Word of God.[144] If you are a believer who knows the Word of God, then you know this truth. A baby in the womb of his or her mother is not an enemy a soldier might face of the battlefield or a criminal who committed a capital offense and was found guilty by a jury of his or her peers. If you are a believer who had an abortion, you are not under condemnation. God loves you, unconditionally, and His mercy is great. If you know of someone contemplating abortion, share the Truth of God's Word. Tell them to *"Choose Life!"* And always remember God's wonderful commentary on the effect of His Word in Isaiah 55:11, *"So shall my word be that goeth forth out of my mouth: it shall not return unto me void, but it shall accomplish that which I please, and it shall prosper in the thing whereto I sent it."* We all benefit and prosper with the knowledge of, and adherence to, the Word of God!

If you are a follower of the Lord Jesus Christ, and know His Word, there is no debate. Choose Life!

~~~~~~~~~~

"Thou shalt not kill."
~~~ Exodus 20:13

---

[144] Exodus 20:13; Deuteronomy 5:17; Matthew 5:21; Romans 13:9.

Chapter 17

The Book of John

~ ~ ~ ~ ~

"And the light shineth in darkness; and the darkness comprehended it not."
~~~ John 1:5

"For God so loved the world, that he gave his only begotten Son,
that whosoever believeth in him should not perish, but have everlasting life."
~~~ John 3:16

"Ye are my friends, if ye do whatsoever I command you. Henceforth
I call you not servants; for the servant knoweth not what his lord doeth:
but I have called you friends;
for all things that I have heard of my Father I have made known unto you.
Ye have not chosen me, but I have chosen you, and ordained you,
that ye should go and bring forth fruit, and that your fruit should remain:
that whatsoever ye shall ask of the Father in my name, he may give it you."
~~~ John 15:14-16

"And in that day ye shall ask me nothing. Verily, verily, I say unto you,
Whatsoever ye shall ask the Father in my name, he will give it you.
Hitherto have ye asked nothing in my name:
ask, and ye shall receive, that your joy may be full."
~~~ John 16:23-24

~ ~ ~ ~ ~

The Book of John is the fourth book of the Gospels, and is unique in several respects. I mention it more in this work than any other book of the Holy Bible. It was written by John the apostle, who was inspired by the Holy Spirit to write not just this important book, but three epistles and the Book of Revelation. John, along with Peter and James, was regarded as one of the closest disciples to the Lord Jesus Christ. The Book of John was the last of the four Gospels to be written, sometime after the destruction of Jerusalem in 70 A.D. and before John's exile to the island of Patmos.

The Book of John has unique significance in that it expressly notes the existence of Jesus with the Father and the Holy Spirit, before the foundations of the world. And this existence was in Love, Grace, and eternal life.[145] It also describes more miracles than the other Gospels, and provides verbatim declarations by Christ himself on the nature of His divinity and our only path to salvation.

The Book of John is an excellent starting point to unlocking the keys to a godly, abundant life, and clearly understanding the true meaning of our existence. But even with that said, as 2 Timothy 3:16-17 notes, *"[16]All scripture is given by inspiration of God, and is profitable for doctrine, for reproof, for correction, for instruction in righteousness: [17]That the man of God may be perfect, thoroughly furnished unto all good works."* It is with this understanding that I humbly suggest the following reading of John, for the purpose of opening the door to a more intimate and personal relationship with our Lord. As John 1:1 declares, *"In the beginning was the Word, and the Word was with God, and the Word was God."*

I present the Book of John in this work for the purpose of sharing the saving grace of our Lord, and I do so in the text of the King James Version (KJV) of the Holy Bible. This version, in my opinion, is the most accurate and complete text of Holy Scripture. The KJV was first transcribed in 1611 A.D., more than 400 years ago, authorized by order of a King, and it was the first such undertaking by a head of state since the first Christian Roman Emperor, Constantine, did so in 325 A.D., when he summoned the First Council of Nicaea, which gathered together Holy Scripture and

---

[145] John 17:5, 24.

instituted the Nicene Creed.[146]   The KJV also puts to rest any question of the Trinity, as 1 John 5:7 states, *"For there are three that bear record in heaven, the Father, the Word, and the Holy Ghost: and these three are one."* You will not find this verse of Truth or a multitude of others in the NIV or the NASB or many other modern translations.   Nor will you find the express words of the Lord regarding victory in spiritual warfare in the NIV, particularly when He rebuked the devil and cast him out of a child;[147] when the apostles asked Him why they could not cast out the devil,[148] Jesus shares the power of faith[149] and declares in Matthew 17:21 of the KJV, *"Howbeit this kind goeth not out but by prayer and fasting."* Prayer and fasting are an essential part of our walk.   And it gives me pause to read any other version of Holy Scripture regarding the lineage of Christ Jesus in Hosea 11:12: The KJV states, *"Ephraim compasseth me about with lies, and the house of Israel with deceit:*

---

[146] First Council of Nicaea (325 A.D.): *"We believe in one God, the Father Almighty, Maker of all things visible and invisible. And in one **Lord** Jesus Christ, the Son of God, begotten of the Father [the only-begotten; that is, of the essence of the Father, God of God], Light of Light, very God of very God, begotten, not made, being of one substance with the Father; whom all things were made [both in heaven and on earth]; Who for us men, and for our salvation, came down and was incarnate and was made man; He suffered, and the third day he rose again, ascended into heaven; From thence he shall come to judge the quick and the dead. And in the Holy Ghost."*
First Council of Constantinople (381 A.D.): *"We believe in one God, the Father Almighty, Maker of heaven and earth, and of all things visible and invisible. And in one Lord Jesus Christ, the only-begotten Son of God, begotten of the Father before all worlds (æons), Light of Light, very God of very God, begotten, not made, being of one substance with the Father; by whom all things were made; who for us men, and for our salvation, came down from heaven, and was incarnate by the Holy Ghost of the Virgin Mary, and was made man; he was crucified for us under Pontius Pilate, and suffered, and was buried, and the third day he rose again, according to the Scriptures, and ascended into heaven, and sitteth on the right hand of the Father; from thence he shall come again, with glory, to judge the quick and the dead; whose kingdom shall have no end. And in the Holy Ghost, the Lord and Giver of life, who proceedeth from the Father, who with the Father and the Son together is worshiped and glorified, who spake by the prophets. In one holy catholic and apostolic Church; we acknowledge one baptism for the remission of sins; we look for the resurrection of the dead, and the life of the world to come. Amen."*

[147] Matthew 17:18.
[148] Matthew 17:19.
[149] Matthew 17:20.

but Judah yet ruleth with God, and is faithful with the saints." And the NKJV, to its credit, likewise notes "*... But Judah still walks with God, Even with the Holy One who is faithful.*" This description of Judah is faithful and with God. However, the NASB notes the same verse as, "**... Judah is also unruly against God, Even against the Holy One who is faithful.**" In the NASB, as well as the NIV, Judah is described as *"unruly"* and the enemy of God. This diametrically opposite characterization of Judah is also found in other versions. Remember, Jesus is called *"the Lion of the tribe of Judah, the Root of David."*[150] Jesus is always faithful,[151] without exception. He is God.[152] And as the KJV of Hosea 11:12 declares, "**Judah yet ruleth with God, and is faithful with the saints.**" The other versions are problematic in describing the character of the lineage of our Saviour. But whether you were first educated in your walk as a Christian through the KJV or some other version, it is my hope and prayer that you will seek His truth, have discernment, and are guided in your walk of faith with your eyes and ears wide open, free of deceit and false doctrine, and submitting yourself to the Spirit of God.

With that said, behold the Book of John: A wonderful gateway to the greatest journey of anyone's life, a personal journey to discover power, success, and eternal joy. It is the path to the Way, the Truth, and the Life.[153] It is the Way to living a godly life. This is the Word of God ...

---

[150] Revelation 5:5.
[151] Deuteronomy 7:9; Psalm 89:8; 1 Corinthians 1:9; 1 Corinthians 10:13.
[152] John 14:9; John 17:11; 1 Corinthians 8:6; 1 John 5:7.
[153] John 14:6.

John 1

[1] In the beginning was the Word, and the Word was with God, and the Word was God.

[2] The same was in the beginning with God.

[3] All things were made by him; and without him was not any thing made that was made.

[4] In him was life; and the life was the light of men.

[5] And the light shineth in darkness; and the darkness comprehended it not.

[6] There was a man sent from God, whose name was John.

[7] The same came for a witness, to bear witness of the Light, that all men through him might believe.

[8] He was not that Light, but was sent to bear witness of that Light.

[9] That was the true Light, which lighteth every man that cometh into the world.

[10] He was in the world, and the world was made by him, and the world knew him not.

[11] He came unto his own, and his own received him not.

[12] But as many as received him, to them gave he power to become the sons of God, even to them that believe on his name:

[13] Which were born, not of blood, nor of the will of the flesh, nor of the will of man, but of God.

[14] And the Word was made flesh, and dwelt among us, (and we beheld his glory, the glory as of the only begotten of the Father,) full of grace and truth.

[15] John bare witness of him, and cried, saying, This was he of whom I spake, He that cometh after me is preferred before me: for he was before me.

[16] And of his fulness have all we received, and grace for grace.

[17] For the law was given by Moses, but grace and truth came by Jesus Christ.

[18] No man hath seen God at any time; the only begotten Son, which is in the bosom of the Father, he hath declared him.

[19] And this is the record of John, when the Jews sent priests and Levites from Jerusalem to ask him, Who art thou?

[20] And he confessed, and denied not; but confessed, I am not the Christ.

[21] And they asked him, What then? Art thou Elias? And he saith, I am not. Art thou that prophet? And he answered, No.

[22] Then said they unto him, Who art thou? that we may give an answer to them that sent us. What sayest thou of thyself?

[23] He said, I am the voice of one crying in the wilderness, Make straight the way of the Lord, as said the prophet Esaias.

[24] And they which were sent were of the Pharisees.

[25] And they asked him, and said unto him, Why baptizest thou then, if thou be not that Christ, nor Elias, neither that prophet?

[26] John answered them, saying, I baptize with water: but there standeth one among you, whom ye know not;

[27] He it is, who coming after me is preferred before me, whose shoe's latchet I am not worthy to unloose.

[28] These things were done in Bethabara beyond Jordan, where John was baptizing.

[29] The next day John seeth Jesus coming unto him, and saith, Behold the Lamb of God, which taketh away the sin of the world.

[30] This is he of whom I said, After me cometh a man which is preferred before me: for he was before me.

[31] And I knew him not: but that he should be made manifest to Israel, therefore am I come baptizing with water.

[32] And John bare record, saying, I saw the Spirit descending from heaven like a dove, and it abode upon him.

[33] And I knew him not: but he that sent me to baptize with water, the same said unto me, Upon whom thou shalt see the Spirit descending, and remaining on him, the same is he which baptizeth with the Holy Ghost.

[34] And I saw, and bare record that this is the Son of God.

[35] Again the next day after John stood, and two of his disciples;

[36] And looking upon Jesus as he walked, he saith, Behold the Lamb of God!

[37] And the two disciples heard him speak, and they followed Jesus.

[38] Then Jesus turned, and saw them following, and saith unto

them, What seek ye? They said unto him, Rabbi, (which is to say, being interpreted, Master,) where dwellest thou?

[**39**] He saith unto them, Come and see. They came and saw where he dwelt, and abode with him that day: for it was about the tenth hour.

[**40**] One of the two which heard John speak, and followed him, was Andrew, Simon Peter's brother.

[**41**] He first findeth his own brother Simon, and saith unto him, We have found the Messias, which is, being interpreted, the Christ.

[**42**] And he brought him to Jesus. And when Jesus beheld him, he said, Thou art Simon the son of Jona: thou shalt be called Cephas, which is by interpretation, A stone.

[**43**] The day following Jesus would go forth into Galilee, and findeth Philip, and saith unto him, Follow me.

[**44**] Now Philip was of Bethsaida, the city of Andrew and Peter.

[**45**] Philip findeth Nathanael, and saith unto him, We have found him, of whom Moses in the law, and the prophets, did write, Jesus of Nazareth, the son of Joseph.

[**46**] And Nathanael said unto him, Can there any good thing come out of Nazareth? Philip saith unto him, Come and see.

[**47**] Jesus saw Nathanael coming to him, and saith of him, Behold an Israelite indeed, in whom is no guile!

[**48**] Nathanael saith unto him, Whence knowest thou me? Jesus answered and said unto him, Before that Philip called thee, when thou wast under the fig tree, I saw thee.

[**49**] Nathanael answered and saith unto him, Rabbi, thou art the Son of God; thou art the King of Israel.

[**50**] Jesus answered and said unto him, Because I said unto thee, I saw thee under the fig tree, believest thou? thou shalt see greater things than these.

[**51**] And he saith unto him, Verily, verily, I say unto you, Hereafter ye shall see heaven open, and the angels of God ascending and descending upon the Son of man.

John 2

[1] And the third day there was a marriage in Cana of Galilee; and the mother of Jesus was there:

[2] And both Jesus was called, and his disciples, to the marriage.

[3] And when they wanted wine, the mother of Jesus saith unto him, They have no wine.

[4] Jesus saith unto her, Woman, what have I to do with thee? mine hour is not yet come.

[5] His mother saith unto the servants, Whatsoever he saith unto you, do it.

[6] And there were set there six waterpots of stone, after the manner of the purifying of the Jews, containing two or three firkins apiece.

[7] Jesus saith unto them, Fill the waterpots with water. And they filled them up to the brim.

[8] And he saith unto them, Draw out now, and bear unto the governor of the feast. And they bare it.

[9] When the ruler of the feast had tasted the water that was made wine, and knew not whence it was: (but the servants which drew the water knew;) the governor of the feast called the bridegroom,

[10] And saith unto him, Every man at the beginning doth set forth good wine; and when men have well drunk, then that which is worse: but thou hast kept the good wine until now.

[11] This beginning of miracles did Jesus in Cana of Galilee, and manifested forth his glory; and his disciples believed on him.

[12] After this he went down to Capernaum, he, and his mother, and his brethren, and his disciples: and they continued there not many days.

[13] And the Jews' passover was at hand, and Jesus went up to Jerusalem,

[14] And found in the temple those that sold oxen and sheep and doves, and the changers of money sitting:

[15] And when he had made a scourge of small cords, he drove them all out of the temple, and the sheep, and the oxen; and poured out the changers' money, and overthrew the tables;

[16] And said unto them that sold doves, Take these things hence; make not my Father's house an house of merchandise.

[17] And his disciples remembered that it was written, The zeal of thine house hath eaten me up.

[18] Then answered the Jews and said unto him, What sign shewest thou unto us, seeing that thou doest these things?

[19] Jesus answered and said unto them, Destroy this temple, and in three days I will raise it up.

[20] Then said the Jews, Forty and six years was this temple in building, and wilt thou rear it up in three days?

[21] But he spake of the temple of his body.

[22] When therefore he was risen from the dead, his disciples remembered that he had said this unto them; and they believed the scripture, and the word which Jesus had said.

[23] Now when he was in Jerusalem at the passover, in the feast day, many believed in his name, when they saw the miracles which he did.

[24] But Jesus did not commit himself unto them, because he knew all men,

[25] And needed not that any should testify of man: for he knew what was in man.

John 3

[1] There was a man of the Pharisees, named Nicodemus, a ruler of the Jews:

[2] The same came to Jesus by night, and said unto him, Rabbi, we know that thou art a teacher come from God: for no man can do these miracles that thou doest, except God be with him.

[3] Jesus answered and said unto him, Verily, verily, I say unto thee, Except a man be born again, he cannot see the kingdom of God.

[4] Nicodemus saith unto him, How can a man be born when he is old? can he enter the second time into his mother's womb, and be born?

[5] Jesus answered, Verily, verily, I say unto thee, Except a man be born of water and of the Spirit, he cannot enter into the kingdom of God.

[6] That which is born of the flesh is flesh; and that which is born of the Spirit is spirit.

[7] Marvel not that I said unto thee, Ye must be born again.

[8] The wind bloweth where it listeth, and thou hearest the sound thereof, but canst not tell whence it cometh, and whither it goeth: so is every one that is born of the Spirit.

[9] Nicodemus answered and said unto him, How can these things be?

[10] Jesus answered and said unto him, Art thou a master of Israel, and knowest not these things?

[11] Verily, verily, I say unto thee, We speak that we do know, and testify that we have seen; and ye receive not our witness.

[12] If I have told you earthly things, and ye believe not, how shall ye believe, if I tell you of heavenly things?

[13] And no man hath ascended up to heaven, but he that came down from heaven, even the Son of man which is in heaven.

[14] And as Moses lifted up the serpent in the wilderness, even so must the Son of man be lifted up:

[15] That whosoever believeth in him should not perish, but have eternal life.

[16] For God so loved the world, that he gave his only begotten Son, that whosoever believeth in him should not perish, but have everlasting life.

[17] For God sent not his Son into the world to condemn the world; but that the world through him might be saved.

[18] He that believeth on him is not condemned: but he that believeth not is condemned already, because he hath not believed in the name of the only begotten Son of God.

[19] And this is the condemnation, that light is come into the world, and men loved darkness rather than light, because their deeds were evil.

[20] For every one that doeth evil hateth the light, neither cometh to the light, lest his deeds should be reproved.

[21] But he that doeth truth cometh to the light, that his deeds may be made manifest, that they are wrought in God.

[22] After these things came Jesus and his disciples into the land of Judaea; and there he tarried with them, and baptized.

[23] And John also was baptizing in Aenon near to Salim, because there was much water there: and they came, and were baptized.

[24] For John was not yet cast into prison.

[25] Then there arose a question between some of John's disciples and the Jews about purifying.

[26] And they came unto John, and said unto him, Rabbi, he that was with thee beyond Jordan, to whom thou barest witness, behold, the same baptizeth, and all men come to him.

[27] John answered and said, A man can receive nothing, except it be given him from heaven.

[28] Ye yourselves bear me witness, that I said, I am not the Christ, but that I am sent before him.

[29] He that hath the bride is the bridegroom: but the friend of the bridegroom, which standeth and heareth him, rejoiceth greatly because of the bridegroom's voice: this my joy therefore is fulfilled.

[30] He must increase, but I must decrease.

[31] He that cometh from above is above all: he that is of the earth is earthly, and speaketh of the earth: he that cometh from heaven is above all.

[32] And what he hath seen and heard, that he testifieth; and no man receiveth his testimony.

[33] He that hath received his testimony hath set to his seal that God is true.

[34] For he whom God hath sent speaketh the words of God: for God giveth not the Spirit by measure unto him.

[35] The Father loveth the Son, and hath given all things into his hand.

[36] He that believeth on the Son hath everlasting life: and he that believeth not the Son shall not see life; but the wrath of God abideth on him.

John 4

[1] When therefore the Lord knew how the Pharisees had heard that Jesus made and baptized more disciples than John,

[2] (Though Jesus himself baptized not, but his disciples,)

[3] He left Judaea, and departed again into Galilee.

[4] And he must needs go through Samaria.

[5] Then cometh he to a city of Samaria, which is called Sychar, near to the parcel of ground that Jacob gave to his son Joseph.

[6] Now Jacob's well was there. Jesus therefore, being wearied with his journey, sat thus on the well: and it was about the sixth hour.

[7] There cometh a woman of Samaria to draw water: Jesus saith unto her, Give me to drink.

[8] (For his disciples were gone away unto the city to buy meat.)

[9] Then saith the woman of Samaria unto him, How is it that thou, being a Jew, askest drink of me, which am a woman of Samaria? for the Jews have no dealings with the Samaritans.

[10] Jesus answered and said unto her, If thou knewest the gift of God, and who it is that saith to thee, Give me to drink; thou wouldest have asked of him, and he would have given thee living water.

[11] The woman saith unto him, Sir, thou hast nothing to draw with, and the well is deep: from whence then hast thou that living water?

[12] Art thou greater than our father Jacob, which gave us the well, and drank thereof himself, and his children, and his cattle?

[13] Jesus answered and said unto her, Whosoever drinketh of this water shall thirst again:

[14] But whosoever drinketh of the water that I shall give him shall never thirst; but the water that I shall give him shall be in him a well of water springing up into everlasting life.

[15] The woman saith unto him, Sir, give me this water, that I thirst not, neither come hither to draw.

[16] Jesus saith unto her, Go, call thy husband, and come hither.

[17] The woman answered and said, I have no husband. Jesus said unto her, Thou hast well said, I have no husband:

[18] For thou hast had five husbands; and he whom thou now hast is not thy husband: in that saidst thou truly.

[19] The woman saith unto him, Sir, I perceive that thou art a prophet.

[20] Our fathers worshipped in this mountain; and ye say, that in Jerusalem is the place where men ought to worship.

[21] Jesus saith unto her, Woman, believe me, the hour cometh, when ye shall neither in this mountain, nor yet at Jerusalem, worship the Father.

[22] Ye worship ye know not what: we know what we worship: for salvation is of the Jews.

[23] But the hour cometh, and now is, when the true worshippers shall worship the Father in spirit and in truth: for the Father seeketh such to worship him.

[24] God is a Spirit: and they that worship him must worship him in spirit and in truth.

[25] The woman saith unto him, I know that Messias cometh, which is called Christ: when he is come, he will tell us all things.

[26] Jesus saith unto her, I that speak unto thee am he.

[27] And upon this came his disciples, and marvelled that he talked with the woman: yet no man said, What seekest thou? or, Why talkest thou with her?

[28] The woman then left her waterpot, and went her way into the city, and saith to the men,

[29] Come, see a man, which told me all things that ever I did: is not this the Christ?

[30] Then they went out of the city, and came unto him.

[31] In the mean while his disciples prayed him, saying, Master, eat.

[32] But he said unto them, I have meat to eat that ye know not of.

[33] Therefore said the disciples one to another, Hath any man brought him ought to eat?

[34] Jesus saith unto them, My meat is to do the will of him that sent me, and to finish his work.

[35] Say not ye, There are yet four months, and then cometh harvest? behold, I say unto you, Lift up your eyes, and look on the fields; for they are white already to harvest.

[36] And he that reapeth receiveth wages, and gathereth fruit unto life eternal: that both he that soweth and he that reapeth may rejoice together.

[37] And herein is that saying true, One soweth, and another reapeth.

[38] I sent you to reap that whereon ye bestowed no labour: other men laboured, and ye are entered into their labours.

[39] And many of the Samaritans of that city believed on him for the saying of the woman, which testified, He told me all that ever I did.

[40] So when the Samaritans were come unto him, they besought him that he would tarry with them: and he abode there two days.

[41] And many more believed because of his own word;

[42] And said unto the woman, Now we believe, not because of thy saying: for we have heard him ourselves, and know that this is indeed the Christ, the Saviour of the world.

[43] Now after two days he departed thence, and went into Galilee.

[44] For Jesus himself testified, that a prophet hath no honour in his own country.

[45] Then when he was come into Galilee, the Galilaeans received him, having seen all the things that he did at Jerusalem at the feast: for they also went unto the feast.

[46] So Jesus came again into Cana of Galilee, where he made the water wine. And there was a certain nobleman, whose son was sick at Capernaum.

[47] When he heard that Jesus was come out of Judaea into Galilee, he went unto him, and besought him that he would come down, and heal his son: for he was at the point of death.

[48] Then said Jesus unto him, Except ye see signs and wonders, ye will not believe.

[49] The nobleman saith unto him, Sir, come down ere my child die.

[50] Jesus saith unto him, Go thy way; thy son liveth. And the man believed the word that Jesus had spoken unto him, and he went his way.

[51] And as he was now going down, his servants met him, and told him, saying, Thy son liveth.

[52] Then inquired he of them the hour when he began to amend.

And they said unto him, Yesterday at the seventh hour the fever left him.

[53] So the father knew that it was at the same hour, in the which Jesus said unto him, Thy son liveth: and himself believed, and his whole house.

[54] This is again the second miracle that Jesus did, when he was come out of Judaea into Galilee.

John 5

[1] After this there was a feast of the Jews; and Jesus went up to Jerusalem.

[2] Now there is at Jerusalem by the sheep market a pool, which is called in the Hebrew tongue Bethesda, having five porches.

[3] In these lay a great multitude of impotent folk, of blind, halt, withered, waiting for the moving of the water.

[4] For an angel went down at a certain season into the pool, and troubled the water: whosoever then first after the troubling of the water stepped in was made whole of whatsoever disease he had.

[5] And a certain man was there, which had an infirmity thirty and eight years.

[6] When Jesus saw him lie, and knew that he had been now a long time in that case, he saith unto him, Wilt thou be made whole?

[7] The impotent man answered him, Sir, I have no man, when the water is troubled, to put me into the pool: but while I am coming, another steppeth down before me.

[8] Jesus saith unto him, Rise, take up thy bed, and walk.

[9] And immediately the man was made whole, and took up his bed, and walked: and on the same day was the sabbath.

[10] The Jews therefore said unto him that was cured, It is the sabbath day: it is not lawful for thee to carry thy bed.

[11] He answered them, He that made me whole, the same said unto me, Take up thy bed, and walk.

[12] Then asked they him, What man is that which said unto thee, Take up thy bed, and walk?

[13] And he that was healed wist not who it was: for Jesus had conveyed himself away, a multitude being in that place.

[14] Afterward Jesus findeth him in the temple, and said unto him, Behold, thou art made whole: sin no more, lest a worse thing come unto thee.

[15] The man departed, and told the Jews that it was Jesus, which had made him whole.

[16] And therefore did the Jews persecute Jesus, and sought to slay him, because he had done these things on the sabbath day.

[17] But Jesus answered them, My Father worketh hitherto, and I work.

[18] Therefore the Jews sought the more to kill him, because he not only had broken the sabbath, but said also that God was his Father, making himself equal with God.

[19] Then answered Jesus and said unto them, Verily, verily, I say unto you, The Son can do nothing of himself, but what he seeth the Father do: for what things soever he doeth, these also doeth the Son likewise.

[20] For the Father loveth the Son, and sheweth him all things that himself doeth: and he will shew him greater works than these, that ye may marvel.

[21] For as the Father raiseth up the dead, and quickeneth them; even so the Son quickeneth whom he will.

[22] For the Father judgeth no man, but hath committed all judgment unto the Son:

[23] That all men should honour the Son, even as they honour the Father. He that honoureth not the Son honoureth not the Father which hath sent him.

[24] Verily, verily, I say unto you, He that heareth my word, and believeth on him that sent me, hath everlasting life, and shall not come into condemnation; but is passed from death unto life.

[25] Verily, verily, I say unto you, The hour is coming, and now is, when the dead shall hear the voice of the Son of God: and they that hear shall live.

[26] For as the Father hath life in himself; so hath he given to the Son to have life in himself;

[27] And hath given him authority to execute judgment also, because he is the Son of man.

[28] Marvel not at this: for the hour is coming, in the which all that are in the graves shall hear his voice,

[29] And shall come forth; they that have done good, unto the resurrection of life; and they that have done evil, unto the resurrection of damnation.

[30] I can of mine own self do nothing: as I hear, I judge: and my judgment is just; because I seek not mine own will, but the will of the Father which hath sent me.

[31] If I bear witness of myself, my witness is not true.

[32] There is another that beareth witness of me; and I know that the witness which he witnesseth of me is true.

[33] Ye sent unto John, and he bare witness unto the truth.

[34] But I receive not testimony from man: but these things I say, that ye might be saved.

[35] He was a burning and a shining light: and ye were willing for a season to rejoice in his light.

[36] But I have greater witness than that of John: for the works which the Father hath given me to finish, the same works that I do, bear witness of me, that the Father hath sent me.

[37] And the Father himself, which hath sent me, hath borne witness of me. Ye have neither heard his voice at any time, nor seen his shape.

[38] And ye have not his word abiding in you: for whom he hath sent, him ye believe not.

[39] Search the scriptures; for in them ye think ye have eternal life: and they are they which testify of me.

[40] And ye will not come to me, that ye might have life.

[41] I receive not honour from men.

[42] But I know you, that ye have not the love of God in you.

[43] I am come in my Father's name, and ye receive me not: if another shall come in his own name, him ye will receive.

[44] How can ye believe, which receive honour one of another, and seek not the honour that cometh from God only?

[45] Do not think that I will accuse you to the Father: there is one

that accuseth you, even Moses, in whom ye trust.

[46] For had ye believed Moses, ye would have believed me: for he wrote of me.

[47] But if ye believe not his writings, how shall ye believe my words?

John 6

[1] After these things Jesus went over the sea of Galilee, which is the sea of Tiberias.

[2] And a great multitude followed him, because they saw his miracles which he did on them that were diseased.

[3] And Jesus went up into a mountain, and there he sat with his disciples.

[4] And the passover, a feast of the Jews, was nigh.

[5] When Jesus then lifted up his eyes, and saw a great company come unto him, he saith unto Philip, Whence shall we buy bread, that these may eat?

[6] And this he said to prove him: for he himself knew what he would do.

[7] Philip answered him, Two hundred pennyworth of bread is not sufficient for them, that every one of them may take a little.

[8] One of his disciples, Andrew, Simon Peter's brother, saith unto him,

[9] There is a lad here, which hath five barley loaves, and two small fishes: but what are they among so many?

[10] And Jesus said, Make the men sit down. Now there was much grass in the place. So the men sat down, in number about five thousand.

[11] And Jesus took the loaves; and when he had given thanks, he distributed to the disciples, and the disciples to them that were set down; and likewise of the fishes as much as they would.

[12] When they were filled, he said unto his disciples, Gather up the fragments that remain, that nothing be lost.

[13] Therefore they gathered them together, and filled twelve baskets with the fragments of the five barley loaves, which remained over and above unto them that had eaten.

[14] Then those men, when they had seen the miracle that Jesus did, said, This is of a truth that prophet that should come into the world.

[15] When Jesus therefore perceived that they would come and take him by force, to make him a king, he departed again into a mountain himself alone.

[16] And when even was now come, his disciples went down unto the sea,

[17] And entered into a ship, and went over the sea toward Capernaum. And it was now dark, and Jesus was not come to them.

[18] And the sea arose by reason of a great wind that blew.

[19] So when they had rowed about five and twenty or thirty furlongs, they see Jesus walking on the sea, and drawing nigh unto the ship: and they were afraid.

[20] But he saith unto them, It is I; be not afraid.

[21] Then they willingly received him into the ship: and immediately the ship was at the land whither they went.

[22] The day following, when the people which stood on the other side of the sea saw that there was none other boat there, save that one whereinto his disciples were entered, and that Jesus went not with his disciples into the boat, but that his disciples were gone away alone;

[23] (Howbeit there came other boats from Tiberias nigh unto the place where they did eat bread, after that the Lord had given thanks:)

[24] When the people therefore saw that Jesus was not there, neither his disciples, they also took shipping, and came to Capernaum, seeking for Jesus.

[25] And when they had found him on the other side of the sea, they said unto him, Rabbi, when camest thou hither?

[26] Jesus answered them and said, Verily, verily, I say unto you, Ye seek me, not because ye saw the miracles, but because ye did eat of the loaves, and were filled.

[**27**] Labour not for the meat which perisheth, but for that meat which endureth unto everlasting life, which the Son of man shall give unto you: for him hath God the Father sealed.

[**28**] Then said they unto him, What shall we do, that we might work the works of God?

[**29**] Jesus answered and said unto them, This is the work of God, that ye believe on him whom he hath sent.

[**30**] They said therefore unto him, What sign shewest thou then, that we may see, and believe thee? what dost thou work?

[**31**] Our fathers did eat manna in the desert; as it is written, He gave them bread from heaven to eat.

[**32**] Then Jesus said unto them, Verily, verily, I say unto you, Moses gave you not that bread from heaven; but my Father giveth you the true bread from heaven.

[**33**] For the bread of God is he which cometh down from heaven, and giveth life unto the world.

[**34**] Then said they unto him, Lord, evermore give us this bread.

[**35**] And Jesus said unto them, I am the bread of life: he that cometh to me shall never hunger; and he that believeth on me shall never thirst.

[**36**] But I said unto you, That ye also have seen me, and believe not.

[**37**] All that the Father giveth me shall come to me; and him that cometh to me I will in no wise cast out.

[**38**] For I came down from heaven, not to do mine own will, but the will of him that sent me.

[**39**] And this is the Father's will which hath sent me, that of all which he hath given me I should lose nothing, but should raise it up again at the last day.

[**40**] And this is the will of him that sent me, that every one which seeth the Son, and believeth on him, may have everlasting life: and I will raise him up at the last day.

[**41**] The Jews then murmured at him, because he said, I am the bread which came down from heaven.

[**42**] And they said, Is not this Jesus, the son of Joseph, whose father and mother we know? how is it then that he saith, I came down from heaven?

[43] Jesus therefore answered and said unto them, Murmur not among yourselves.

[44] No man can come to me, except the Father which hath sent me draw him: and I will raise him up at the last day.

[45] It is written in the prophets, And they shall be all taught of God. Every man therefore that hath heard, and hath learned of the Father, cometh unto me.

[46] Not that any man hath seen the Father, save he which is of God, he hath seen the Father.

[47] Verily, verily, I say unto you, He that believeth on me hath everlasting life.

[48] I am that bread of life.

[49] Your fathers did eat manna in the wilderness, and are dead.

[50] This is the bread which cometh down from heaven, that a man may eat thereof, and not die.

[51] I am the living bread which came down from heaven: if any man eat of this bread, he shall live for ever: and the bread that I will give is my flesh, which I will give for the life of the world.

[52] The Jews therefore strove among themselves, saying, How can this man give us his flesh to eat?

[53] Then Jesus said unto them, Verily, verily, I say unto you, Except ye eat the flesh of the Son of man, and drink his blood, ye have no life in you.

[54] Whoso eateth my flesh, and drinketh my blood, hath eternal life; and I will raise him up at the last day.

[55] For my flesh is meat indeed, and my blood is drink indeed.

[56] He that eateth my flesh, and drinketh my blood, dwelleth in me, and I in him.

[57] As the living Father hath sent me, and I live by the Father: so he that eateth me, even he shall live by me.

[58] This is that bread which came down from heaven: not as your fathers did eat manna, and are dead: he that eateth of this bread shall live for ever.

[59] These things said he in the synagogue, as he taught in Capernaum.

[60] Many therefore of his disciples, when they had heard this, said,

This is an hard saying; who can hear it?

[61] When Jesus knew in himself that his disciples murmured at it, he said unto them, Doth this offend you?

[62] What and if ye shall see the Son of man ascend up where he was before?

[63] It is the spirit that quickeneth; the flesh profiteth nothing: the words that I speak unto you, they are spirit, and they are life.

[64] But there are some of you that believe not. For Jesus knew from the beginning who they were that believed not, and who should betray him.

[65] And he said, Therefore said I unto you, that no man can come unto me, except it were given unto him of my Father.

[66] From that time many of his disciples went back, and walked no more with him.

[67] Then said Jesus unto the twelve, Will ye also go away?

[68] Then Simon Peter answered him, Lord, to whom shall we go? thou hast the words of eternal life.

[69] And we believe and are sure that thou art that Christ, the Son of the living God.

[70] Jesus answered them, Have not I chosen you twelve, and one of you is a devil?

[71] He spake of Judas Iscariot the son of Simon: for he it was that should betray him, being one of the twelve.

John 7

[1] After these things Jesus walked in Galilee: for he would not walk in Jewry, because the Jews sought to kill him.

[2] Now the Jews' feast of tabernacles was at hand.

[3] His brethren therefore said unto him, Depart hence, and go into Judaea, that thy disciples also may see the works that thou doest.

[4] For there is no man that doeth any thing in secret, and he himself seeketh to be known openly. If thou do these things, shew thyself to the world.

[5] For neither did his brethren believe in him.

[6] Then Jesus said unto them, My time is not yet come: but your time is alway ready.

[7] The world cannot hate you; but me it hateth, because I testify of it, that the works thereof are evil.

[8] Go ye up unto this feast: I go not up yet unto this feast; for my time is not yet full come.

[9] When he had said these words unto them, he abode still in Galilee.

[10] But when his brethren were gone up, then went he also up unto the feast, not openly, but as it were in secret.

[11] Then the Jews sought him at the feast, and said, Where is he?

[12] And there was much murmuring among the people concerning him: for some said, He is a good man: others said, Nay; but he deceiveth the people.

[13] Howbeit no man spake openly of him for fear of the Jews.

[14] Now about the midst of the feast Jesus went up into the temple, and taught.

[15] And the Jews marvelled, saying, How knoweth this man letters, having never learned?

[16] Jesus answered them, and said, My doctrine is not mine, but his that sent me.

[17] If any man will do his will, he shall know of the doctrine, whether it be of God, or whether I speak of myself.

[18] He that speaketh of himself seeketh his own glory: but he that seeketh his glory that sent him, the same is true, and no unrighteousness is in him.

[19] Did not Moses give you the law, and yet none of you keepeth the law? Why go ye about to kill me?

[20] The people answered and said, Thou hast a devil: who goeth about to kill thee?

[21] Jesus answered and said unto them, I have done one work, and ye all marvel.

[22] Moses therefore gave unto you circumcision; (not because it is of Moses, but of the fathers;) and ye on the sabbath day circumcise a man.

[23] If a man on the sabbath day receive circumcision, that the law

of Moses should not be broken; are ye angry at me, because I have made a man every whit whole on the sabbath day?

[24] Judge not according to the appearance, but judge righteous judgment.

[25] Then said some of them of Jerusalem, Is not this he, whom they seek to kill?

[26] But, lo, he speaketh boldly, and they say nothing unto him. Do the rulers know indeed that this is the very Christ?

[27] Howbeit we know this man whence he is: but when Christ cometh, no man knoweth whence he is.

[28] Then cried Jesus in the temple as he taught, saying, Ye both know me, and ye know whence I am: and I am not come of myself, but he that sent me is true, whom ye know not.

[29] But I know him: for I am from him, and he hath sent me.

[30] Then they sought to take him: but no man laid hands on him, because his hour was not yet come.

[31] And many of the people believed on him, and said, When Christ cometh, will he do more miracles than these which this man hath done?

[32] The Pharisees heard that the people murmured such things concerning him; and the Pharisees and the chief priests sent officers to take him.

[33] Then said Jesus unto them, Yet a little while am I with you, and then I go unto him that sent me.

[34] Ye shall seek me, and shall not find me: and where I am, thither ye cannot come.

[35] Then said the Jews among themselves, Whither will he go, that we shall not find him? will he go unto the dispersed among the Gentiles, and teach the Gentiles?

[36] What manner of saying is this that he said, Ye shall seek me, and shall not find me: and where I am, thither ye cannot come?

[37] In the last day, that great day of the feast, Jesus stood and cried, saying, If any man thirst, let him come unto me, and drink.

[38] He that believeth on me, as the scripture hath said, out of his belly shall flow rivers of living water.

[39] (But this spake he of the Spirit, which they that believe on him

should receive: for the Holy Ghost was not yet given; because that Jesus was not yet glorified.)

[40] Many of the people therefore, when they heard this saying, said, Of a truth this is the Prophet.

[41] Others said, This is the Christ. But some said, Shall Christ come out of Galilee?

[42] Hath not the scripture said, That Christ cometh of the seed of David, and out of the town of Bethlehem, where David was?

[43] So there was a division among the people because of him.

[44] And some of them would have taken him; but no man laid hands on him.

[45] Then came the officers to the chief priests and Pharisees; and they said unto them, Why have ye not brought him?

[46] The officers answered, Never man spake like this man.

[47] Then answered them the Pharisees, Are ye also deceived?

[48] Have any of the rulers or of the Pharisees believed on him?

[49] But this people who knoweth not the law are cursed.

[50] Nicodemus saith unto them, (he that came to Jesus by night, being one of them,)

[51] Doth our law judge any man, before it hear him, and know what he doeth?

[52] They answered and said unto him, Art thou also of Galilee? Search, and look: for out of Galilee ariseth no prophet.

[53] And every man went unto his own house.

John 8

[1] Jesus went unto the mount of Olives.

[2] And early in the morning he came again into the temple, and all the people came unto him; and he sat down, and taught them.

[3] And the scribes and Pharisees brought unto him a woman taken in adultery; and when they had set her in the midst,

[4] They say unto him, Master, this woman was taken in adultery, in the very act.

[**5**] Now Moses in the law commanded us, that such should be stoned: but what sayest thou?

[**6**] This they said, tempting him, that they might have to accuse him. But Jesus stooped down, and with his finger wrote on the ground, as though he heard them not.

[**7**] So when they continued asking him, he lifted up himself, and said unto them, He that is without sin among you, let him first cast a stone at her.

[**8**] And again he stooped down, and wrote on the ground.

[**9**] And they which heard it, being convicted by their own conscience, went out one by one, beginning at the eldest, even unto the last: and Jesus was left alone, and the woman standing in the midst.

[**10**] When Jesus had lifted up himself, and saw none but the woman, he said unto her, Woman, where are those thine accusers? hath no man condemned thee?

[**11**] She said, No man, Lord. And Jesus said unto her, Neither do I condemn thee: go, and sin no more.

[**12**] Then spake Jesus again unto them, saying, I am the light of the world: he that followeth me shall not walk in darkness, but shall have the light of life.

[**13**] The Pharisees therefore said unto him, Thou bearest record of thyself; thy record is not true.

[**14**] Jesus answered and said unto them, Though I bear record of myself, yet my record is true: for I know whence I came, and whither I go; but ye cannot tell whence I come, and whither I go.

[**15**] Ye judge after the flesh; I judge no man.

[**16**] And yet if I judge, my judgment is true: for I am not alone, but I and the Father that sent me.

[**17**] It is also written in your law, that the testimony of two men is true.

[**18**] I am one that bear witness of myself, and the Father that sent me beareth witness of me.

[**19**] Then said they unto him, Where is thy Father? Jesus answered, Ye neither know me, nor my Father: if ye had known me, ye should have known my Father also.

[20] These words spake Jesus in the treasury, as he taught in the temple: and no man laid hands on him; for his hour was not yet come.

[21] Then said Jesus again unto them, I go my way, and ye shall seek me, and shall die in your sins: whither I go, ye cannot come.

[22] Then said the Jews, Will he kill himself? because he saith, Whither I go, ye cannot come.

[23] And he said unto them, Ye are from beneath; I am from above: ye are of this world; I am not of this world.

[24] I said therefore unto you, that ye shall die in your sins: for if ye believe not that I am he, ye shall die in your sins.

[25] Then said they unto him, Who art thou? And Jesus saith unto them, Even the same that I said unto you from the beginning.

[26] I have many things to say and to judge of you: but he that sent me is true; and I speak to the world those things which I have heard of him.

[27] They understood not that he spake to them of the Father.

[28] Then said Jesus unto them, When ye have lifted up the Son of man, then shall ye know that I am he, and that I do nothing of myself; but as my Father hath taught me, I speak these things.

[29] And he that sent me is with me: the Father hath not left me alone; for I do always those things that please him.

[30] As he spake these words, many believed on him.

[31] Then said Jesus to those Jews which believed on him, If ye continue in my word, then are ye my disciples indeed;

[32] And ye shall know the truth, and the truth shall make you free.

[33] They answered him, We be Abraham's seed, and were never in bondage to any man: how sayest thou, Ye shall be made free?

[34] Jesus answered them, Verily, verily, I say unto you, Whosoever committeth sin is the servant of sin.

[35] And the servant abideth not in the house for ever: but the Son abideth ever.

[36] If the Son therefore shall make you free, ye shall be free indeed.

[37] I know that ye are Abraham's seed; but ye seek to kill me, because my word hath no place in you.

[38] I speak that which I have seen with my Father: and ye do that which ye have seen with your father.

[39] They answered and said unto him, Abraham is our father. Jesus saith unto them, If ye were Abraham's children, ye would do the works of Abraham.

[40] But now ye seek to kill me, a man that hath told you the truth, which I have heard of God: this did not Abraham.

[41] Ye do the deeds of your father. Then said they to him, We be not born of fornication; we have one Father, even God.

[42] Jesus said unto them, If God were your Father, ye would love me: for I proceeded forth and came from God; neither came I of myself, but he sent me.

[43] Why do ye not understand my speech? even because ye cannot hear my word.

[44] Ye are of your father the devil, and the lusts of your father ye will do. He was a murderer from the beginning, and abode not in the truth, because there is no truth in him. When he speaketh a lie, he speaketh of his own: for he is a liar, and the father of it.

[45] And because I tell you the truth, ye believe me not.

[46] Which of you convinceth me of sin? And if I say the truth, why do ye not believe me?

[47] He that is of God heareth God's words: ye therefore hear them not, because ye are not of God.

[48] Then answered the Jews, and said unto him, Say we not well that thou art a Samaritan, and hast a devil?

[49] Jesus answered, I have not a devil; but I honour my Father, and ye do dishonour me.

[50] And I seek not mine own glory: there is one that seeketh and judgeth.

[51] Verily, verily, I say unto you, If a man keep my saying, he shall never see death.

[52] Then said the Jews unto him, Now we know that thou hast a devil. Abraham is dead, and the prophets; and thou sayest, If a man keep my saying, he shall never taste of death.

[53] Art thou greater than our father Abraham, which is dead? and the prophets are dead: whom makest thou thyself?

[54] Jesus answered, If I honour myself, my honour is nothing: it is my Father that honoureth me; of whom ye say, that he is your God: [55] Yet ye have not known him; but I know him: and if I should say, I know him not, I shall be a liar like unto you: but I know him, and keep his saying.
[56] Your father Abraham rejoiced to see my day: and he saw it, and was glad.
[57] Then said the Jews unto him, Thou art not yet fifty years old, and hast thou seen Abraham?
[58] Jesus said unto them, Verily, verily, I say unto you, Before Abraham was, I am.
[59] Then took they up stones to cast at him: but Jesus hid himself, and went out of the temple, going through the midst of them, and so passed by.

John 9

[1] And as Jesus passed by, he saw a man which was blind from his birth.
[2] And his disciples asked him, saying, Master, who did sin, this man, or his parents, that he was born blind?
[3] Jesus answered, Neither hath this man sinned, nor his parents: but that the works of God should be made manifest in him.
[4] I must work the works of him that sent me, while it is day: the night cometh, when no man can work.
[5] As long as I am in the world, I am the light of the world.
[6] When he had thus spoken, he spat on the ground, and made clay of the spittle, and he anointed the eyes of the blind man with the clay,
[7] And said unto him, Go, wash in the pool of Siloam, (which is by interpretation, Sent.) He went his way therefore, and washed, and came seeing.
[8] The neighbours therefore, and they which before had seen him that he was blind, said, Is not this he that sat and begged?
[9] Some said, This is he: others said, He is like him: but he said, I am he.

[10] Therefore said they unto him, How were thine eyes opened?
[11] He answered and said, A man that is called Jesus made clay, and anointed mine eyes, and said unto me, Go to the pool of Siloam, and wash: and I went and washed, and I received sight.
[12] Then said they unto him, Where is he? He said, I know not.
[13] They brought to the Pharisees him that aforetime was blind.
[14] And it was the sabbath day when Jesus made the clay, and opened his eyes.
[15] Then again the Pharisees also asked him how he had received his sight. He said unto them, He put clay upon mine eyes, and I washed, and do see.
[16] Therefore said some of the Pharisees, This man is not of God, because he keepeth not the sabbath day. Others said, How can a man that is a sinner do such miracles? And there was a division among them.
[17] They say unto the blind man again, What sayest thou of him, that he hath opened thine eyes? He said, He is a prophet.
[18] But the Jews did not believe concerning him, that he had been blind, and received his sight, until they called the parents of him that had received his sight.
[19] And they asked them, saying, Is this your son, who ye say was born blind? how then doth he now see?
[20] His parents answered them and said, We know that this is our son, and that he was born blind:
[21] But by what means he now seeth, we know not; or who hath opened his eyes, we know not: he is of age; ask him: he shall speak for himself.
[22] These words spake his parents, because they feared the Jews: for the Jews had agreed already, that if any man did confess that he was Christ, he should be put out of the synagogue.
[23] Therefore said his parents, He is of age; ask him.
[24] Then again called they the man that was blind, and said unto him, Give God the praise: we know that this man is a sinner.
[25] He answered and said, Whether he be a sinner or no, I know not: one thing I know, that, whereas I was blind, now I see.
[26] Then said they to him again, What did he to thee? how opened

he thine eyes?

[27] He answered them, I have told you already, and ye did not hear: wherefore would ye hear it again? will ye also be his disciples?

[28] Then they reviled him, and said, Thou art his disciple; but we are Moses' disciples.

[29] We know that God spake unto Moses: as for this fellow, we know not from whence he is.

[30] The man answered and said unto them, Why herein is a marvellous thing, that ye know not from whence he is, and yet he hath opened mine eyes.

[31] Now we know that God heareth not sinners: but if any man be a worshipper of God, and doeth his will, him he heareth.

[32] Since the world began was it not heard that any man opened the eyes of one that was born blind.

[33] If this man were not of God, he could do nothing.

[34] They answered and said unto him, Thou wast altogether born in sins, and dost thou teach us? And they cast him out.

[35] Jesus heard that they had cast him out; and when he had found him, he said unto him, Dost thou believe on the Son of God?

[36] He answered and said, Who is he, Lord, that I might believe on him?

[37] And Jesus said unto him, Thou hast both seen him, and it is he that talketh with thee.

[38] And he said, Lord, I believe. And he worshipped him.

[39] And Jesus said, For judgment I am come into this world, that they which see not might see; and that they which see might be made blind.

[40] And some of the Pharisees which were with him heard these words, and said unto him, Are we blind also?

[41] Jesus said unto them, If ye were blind, ye should have no sin: but now ye say, We see; therefore your sin remaineth.

John 10

[1] Verily, verily, I say unto you, He that entereth not by the door into the sheepfold, but climbeth up some other way, the same is a thief and a robber.

[2] But he that entereth in by the door is the shepherd of the sheep.

[3] To him the porter openeth; and the sheep hear his voice: and he calleth his own sheep by name, and leadeth them out.

[4] And when he putteth forth his own sheep, he goeth before them, and the sheep follow him: for they know his voice.

[5] And a stranger will they not follow, but will flee from him: for they know not the voice of strangers.

[6] This parable spake Jesus unto them: but they understood not what things they were which he spake unto them.

[7] Then said Jesus unto them again, Verily, verily, I say unto you, I am the door of the sheep.

[8] All that ever came before me are thieves and robbers: but the sheep did not hear them.

[9] I am the door: by me if any man enter in, he shall be saved, and shall go in and out, and find pasture.

[10] The thief cometh not, but for to steal, and to kill, and to destroy: I am come that they might have life, and that they might have it more abundantly.

[11] I am the good shepherd: the good shepherd giveth his life for the sheep.

[12] But he that is an hireling, and not the shepherd, whose own the sheep are not, seeth the wolf coming, and leaveth the sheep, and fleeth: and the wolf catcheth them, and scattereth the sheep.

[13] The hireling fleeth, because he is an hireling, and careth not for the sheep.

[14] I am the good shepherd, and know my sheep, and am known of mine.

[15] As the Father knoweth me, even so know I the Father: and I lay down my life for the sheep.

[16] And other sheep I have, which are not of this fold: them also I must bring, and they shall hear my voice; and there shall be one fold, and one shepherd.

[17] Therefore doth my Father love me, because I lay down my life, that I might take it again.

[18] No man taketh it from me, but I lay it down of myself. I have power to lay it down, and I have power to take it again. This commandment have I received of my Father.

[19] There was a division therefore again among the Jews for these sayings.

[20] And many of them said, He hath a devil, and is mad; why hear ye him?

[21] Others said, These are not the words of him that hath a devil. Can a devil open the eyes of the blind?

[22] And it was at Jerusalem the feast of the dedication, and it was winter.

[23] And Jesus walked in the temple in Solomon's porch.

[24] Then came the Jews round about him, and said unto him, How long dost thou make us to doubt? If thou be the Christ, tell us plainly.

[25] Jesus answered them, I told you, and ye believed not: the works that I do in my Father's name, they bear witness of me.

[26] But ye believe not, because ye are not of my sheep, as I said unto you.

[27] My sheep hear my voice, and I know them, and they follow me:

[28] And I give unto them eternal life; and they shall never perish, neither shall any man pluck them out of my hand.

[29] My Father, which gave them me, is greater than all; and no man is able to pluck them out of my Father's hand.

[30] I and my Father are one.

[31] Then the Jews took up stones again to stone him.

[32] Jesus answered them, Many good works have I shewed you from my Father; for which of those works do ye stone me?

[33] The Jews answered him, saying, For a good work we stone thee not; but for blasphemy; and because that thou, being a man, makest thyself God.

[34] Jesus answered them, Is it not written in your law, I said, Ye are gods?

[35] If he called them gods, unto whom the word of God came, and the scripture cannot be broken;

[36] Say ye of him, whom the Father hath sanctified, and sent into the world, Thou blasphemest; because I said, I am the Son of God?

[37] If I do not the works of my Father, believe me not.

[38] But if I do, though ye believe not me, believe the works: that ye may know, and believe, that the Father is in me, and I in him.

[39] Therefore they sought again to take him: but he escaped out of their hand,

[40] And went away again beyond Jordan into the place where John at first baptized; and there he abode.

[41] And many resorted unto him, and said, John did no miracle: but all things that John spake of this man were true.

[42] And many believed on him there.

John 11

[1] Now a certain man was sick, named Lazarus, of Bethany, the town of Mary and her sister Martha.

[2] (It was that Mary which anointed the Lord with ointment, and wiped his feet with her hair, whose brother Lazarus was sick.)

[3] Therefore his sisters sent unto him, saying, Lord, behold, he whom thou lovest is sick.

[4] When Jesus heard that, he said, This sickness is not unto death, but for the glory of God, that the Son of God might be glorified thereby.

[5] Now Jesus loved Martha, and her sister, and Lazarus.

[6] When he had heard therefore that he was sick, he abode two days still in the same place where he was.

[7] Then after that saith he to his disciples, Let us go into Judaea again.

[8] His disciples say unto him, Master, the Jews of late sought to stone thee; and goest thou thither again?

[9] Jesus answered, Are there not twelve hours in the day? If any man walk in the day, he stumbleth not, because he seeth the light of this world.

[10] But if a man walk in the night, he stumbleth, because there is no light in him.

[11] These things said he: and after that he saith unto them, Our friend Lazarus sleepeth; but I go, that I may awake him out of sleep.

[12] Then said his disciples, Lord, if he sleep, he shall do well.

[13] Howbeit Jesus spake of his death: but they thought that he had spoken of taking of rest in sleep.

[14] Then said Jesus unto them plainly, Lazarus is dead.

[15] And I am glad for your sakes that I was not there, to the intent ye may believe; nevertheless let us go unto him.

[16] Then said Thomas, which is called Didymus, unto his fellowdisciples, Let us also go, that we may die with him.

[17] Then when Jesus came, he found that he had lain in the grave four days already.

[18] Now Bethany was nigh unto Jerusalem, about fifteen furlongs off:

[19] And many of the Jews came to Martha and Mary, to comfort them concerning their brother.

[20] Then Martha, as soon as she heard that Jesus was coming, went and met him: but Mary sat still in the house.

[21] Then said Martha unto Jesus, Lord, if thou hadst been here, my brother had not died.

[22] But I know, that even now, whatsoever thou wilt ask of God, God will give it thee.

[23] Jesus saith unto her, Thy brother shall rise again.

[24] Martha saith unto him, I know that he shall rise again in the resurrection at the last day.

[25] Jesus said unto her, I am the resurrection, and the life: he that believeth in me, though he were dead, yet shall he live:

[26] And whosoever liveth and believeth in me shall never die. Believest thou this?

[27] She saith unto him, Yea, Lord: I believe that thou art the Christ, the Son of God, which should come into the world.

[28] And when she had so said, she went her way, and called Mary her sister secretly, saying, The Master is come, and calleth for thee.
[29] As soon as she heard that, she arose quickly, and came unto him.
[30] Now Jesus was not yet come into the town, but was in that place where Martha met him.
[31] The Jews then which were with her in the house, and comforted her, when they saw Mary, that she rose up hastily and went out, followed her, saying, She goeth unto the grave to weep there.
[32] Then when Mary was come where Jesus was, and saw him, she fell down at his feet, saying unto him, Lord, if thou hadst been here, my brother had not died.
[33] When Jesus therefore saw her weeping, and the Jews also weeping which came with her, he groaned in the spirit, and was troubled,
[34] And said, Where have ye laid him? They said unto him, Lord, come and see.
[35] Jesus wept.
[36] Then said the Jews, Behold how he loved him!
[37] And some of them said, Could not this man, which opened the eyes of the blind, have caused that even this man should not have died?
[38] Jesus therefore again groaning in himself cometh to the grave. It was a cave, and a stone lay upon it.
[39] Jesus said, Take ye away the stone. Martha, the sister of him that was dead, saith unto him, Lord, by this time he stinketh: for he hath been dead four days.
[40] Jesus saith unto her, Said I not unto thee, that, if thou wouldest believe, thou shouldest see the glory of God?
[41] Then they took away the stone from the place where the dead was laid. And Jesus lifted up his eyes, and said, Father, I thank thee that thou hast heard me.
[42] And I knew that thou hearest me always: but because of the people which stand by I said it, that they may believe that thou hast sent me.

[**43**] And when he thus had spoken, he cried with a loud voice, Lazarus, come forth.

[**44**] And he that was dead came forth, bound hand and foot with graveclothes: and his face was bound about with a napkin. Jesus saith unto them, Loose him, and let him go.

[**45**] Then many of the Jews which came to Mary, and had seen the things which Jesus did, believed on him.

[**46**] But some of them went their ways to the Pharisees, and told them what things Jesus had done.

[**47**] Then gathered the chief priests and the Pharisees a council, and said, What do we? for this man doeth many miracles.

[**48**] If we let him thus alone, all men will believe on him: and the Romans shall come and take away both our place and nation.

[**49**] And one of them, named Caiaphas, being the high priest that same year, said unto them, Ye know nothing at all,

[**50**] Nor consider that it is expedient for us, that one man should die for the people, and that the whole nation perish not.

[**51**] And this spake he not of himself: but being high priest that year, he prophesied that Jesus should die for that nation;

[**52**] And not for that nation only, but that also he should gather together in one the children of God that were scattered abroad.

[**53**] Then from that day forth they took counsel together for to put him to death.

[**54**] Jesus therefore walked no more openly among the Jews; but went thence unto a country near to the wilderness, into a city called Ephraim, and there continued with his disciples.

[**55**] And the Jews' passover was nigh at hand: and many went out of the country up to Jerusalem before the passover, to purify themselves.

[**56**] Then sought they for Jesus, and spake among themselves, as they stood in the temple, What think ye, that he will not come to the feast?

[**57**] Now both the chief priests and the Pharisees had given a commandment, that, if any man knew where he were, he should shew it, that they might take him.

John 12

[1] Then Jesus six days before the passover came to Bethany, where Lazarus was which had been dead, whom he raised from the dead.
[2] There they made him a supper; and Martha served: but Lazarus was one of them that sat at the table with him.
[3] Then took Mary a pound of ointment of spikenard, very costly, and anointed the feet of Jesus, and wiped his feet with her hair: and the house was filled with the odour of the ointment.
[4] Then saith one of his disciples, Judas Iscariot, Simon's son, which should betray him,
[5] Why was not this ointment sold for three hundred pence, and given to the poor?
[6] This he said, not that he cared for the poor; but because he was a thief, and had the bag, and bare what was put therein.
[7] Then said Jesus, Let her alone: against the day of my burying hath she kept this.
[8] For the poor always ye have with you; but me ye have not always.
[9] Much people of the Jews therefore knew that he was there: and they came not for Jesus' sake only, but that they might see Lazarus also, whom he had raised from the dead.
[10] But the chief priests consulted that they might put Lazarus also to death;
[11] Because that by reason of him many of the Jews went away, and believed on Jesus.
[12] On the next day much people that were come to the feast, when they heard that Jesus was coming to Jerusalem,
[13] Took branches of palm trees, and went forth to meet him, and cried, Hosanna: Blessed is the King of Israel that cometh in the name of the Lord.
[14] And Jesus, when he had found a young ass, sat thereon; as it is written,
[15] Fear not, daughter of Sion: behold, thy King cometh, sitting on an ass's colt.

[**16**] These things understood not his disciples at the first: but when Jesus was glorified, then remembered they that these things were written of him, and that they had done these things unto him.

[**17**] The people therefore that was with him when he called Lazarus out of his grave, and raised him from the dead, bare record.

[**18**] For this cause the people also met him, for that they heard that he had done this miracle.

[**19**] The Pharisees therefore said among themselves, Perceive ye how ye prevail nothing? behold, the world is gone after him.

[**20**] And there were certain Greeks among them that came up to worship at the feast:

[**21**] The same came therefore to Philip, which was of Bethsaida of Galilee, and desired him, saying, Sir, we would see Jesus.

[**22**] Philip cometh and telleth Andrew: and again Andrew and Philip tell Jesus.

[**23**] And Jesus answered them, saying, The hour is come, that the Son of man should be glorified.

[**24**] Verily, verily, I say unto you, Except a corn of wheat fall into the ground and die, it abideth alone: but if it die, it bringeth forth much fruit.

[**25**] He that loveth his life shall lose it; and he that hateth his life in this world shall keep it unto life eternal.

[**26**] If any man serve me, let him follow me; and where I am, there shall also my servant be: if any man serve me, him will my Father honour.

[**27**] Now is my soul troubled; and what shall I say? Father, save me from this hour: but for this cause came I unto this hour.

[**28**] Father, glorify thy name. Then came there a voice from heaven, saying, I have both glorified it, and will glorify it again.

[**29**] The people therefore, that stood by, and heard it, said that it thundered: others said, An angel spake to him.

[**30**] Jesus answered and said, This voice came not because of me, but for your sakes.

[**31**] Now is the judgment of this world: now shall the prince of this world be cast out.

[**32**] And I, if I be lifted up from the earth, will draw all men unto

me.

[33] This he said, signifying what death he should die.

[34] The people answered him, We have heard out of the law that Christ abideth for ever: and how sayest thou, The Son of man must be lifted up? who is this Son of man?

[35] Then Jesus said unto them, Yet a little while is the light with you. Walk while ye have the light, lest darkness come upon you: for he that walketh in darkness knoweth not whither he goeth.

[36] While ye have light, believe in the light, that ye may be the children of light. These things spake Jesus, and departed, and did hide himself from them.

[37] But though he had done so many miracles before them, yet they believed not on him:

[38] That the saying of Esaias the prophet might be fulfilled, which he spake, Lord, who hath believed our report? and to whom hath the arm of the Lord been revealed?

[39] Therefore they could not believe, because that Esaias said again,

[40] He hath blinded their eyes, and hardened their heart; that they should not see with their eyes, nor understand with their heart, and be converted, and I should heal them.

[41] These things said Esaias, when he saw his glory, and spake of him.

[42] Nevertheless among the chief rulers also many believed on him; but because of the Pharisees they did not confess him, lest they should be put out of the synagogue:

[43] For they loved the praise of men more than the praise of God.

[44] Jesus cried and said, He that believeth on me, believeth not on me, but on him that sent me.

[45] And he that seeth me seeth him that sent me.

[46] I am come a light into the world, that whosoever believeth on me should not abide in darkness.

[47] And if any man hear my words, and believe not, I judge him not: for I came not to judge the world, but to save the world.

[48] He that rejecteth me, and receiveth not my words, hath one that judgeth him: the word that I have spoken, the same shall judge

him in the last day.

[**49**] For I have not spoken of myself; but the Father which sent me, he gave me a commandment, what I should say, and what I should speak.

[**50**] And I know that his commandment is life everlasting: whatsoever I speak therefore, even as the Father said unto me, so I speak.

John 13

[**1**] Now before the feast of the passover, when Jesus knew that his hour was come that he should depart out of this world unto the Father, having loved his own which were in the world, he loved them unto the end.

[**2**] And supper being ended, the devil having now put into the heart of Judas Iscariot, Simon's son, to betray him;

[**3**] Jesus knowing that the Father had given all things into his hands, and that he was come from God, and went to God;

[**4**] He riseth from supper, and laid aside his garments; and took a towel, and girded himself.

[**5**] After that he poureth water into a bason, and began to wash the disciples' feet, and to wipe them with the towel wherewith he was girded.

[**6**] Then cometh he to Simon Peter: and Peter saith unto him, Lord, dost thou wash my feet?

[**7**] Jesus answered and said unto him, What I do thou knowest not now; but thou shalt know hereafter.

[**8**] Peter saith unto him, Thou shalt never wash my feet. Jesus answered him, If I wash thee not, thou hast no part with me.

[**9**] Simon Peter saith unto him, Lord, not my feet only, but also my hands and my head.

[**10**] Jesus saith to him, He that is washed needeth not save to wash his feet, but is clean every whit: and ye are clean, but not all.

[**11**] For he knew who should betray him; therefore said he, Ye are not all clean.

[12] So after he had washed their feet, and had taken his garments, and was set down again, he said unto them, Know ye what I have done to you?

[13] Ye call me Master and Lord: and ye say well; for so I am.

[14] If I then, your Lord and Master, have washed your feet; ye also ought to wash one another's feet.

[15] For I have given you an example, that ye should do as I have done to you.

[16] Verily, verily, I say unto you, The servant is not greater than his lord; neither he that is sent greater than he that sent him.

[17] If ye know these things, happy are ye if ye do them.

[18] I speak not of you all: I know whom I have chosen: but that the scripture may be fulfilled, He that eateth bread with me hath lifted up his heel against me.

[19] Now I tell you before it come, that, when it is come to pass, ye may believe that I am he.

[20] Verily, verily, I say unto you, He that receiveth whomsoever I send receiveth me; and he that receiveth me receiveth him that sent me.

[21] When Jesus had thus said, he was troubled in spirit, and testified, and said, Verily, verily, I say unto you, that one of you shall betray me.

[22] Then the disciples looked one on another, doubting of whom he spake.

[23] Now there was leaning on Jesus' bosom one of his disciples, whom Jesus loved.

[24] Simon Peter therefore beckoned to him, that he should ask who it should be of whom he spake.

[25] He then lying on Jesus' breast saith unto him, Lord, who is it?

[26] Jesus answered, He it is, to whom I shall give a sop, when I have dipped it. And when he had dipped the sop, he gave it to Judas Iscariot, the son of Simon.

[27] And after the sop Satan entered into him. Then said Jesus unto him, That thou doest, do quickly.

[28] Now no man at the table knew for what intent he spake this unto him.

[29] For some of them thought, because Judas had the bag, that Jesus had said unto him, Buy those things that we have need of against the feast; or, that he should give something to the poor.
[30] He then having received the sop went immediately out: and it was night.
[31] Therefore, when he was gone out, Jesus said, Now is the Son of man glorified, and God is glorified in him.
[32] If God be glorified in him, God shall also glorify him in himself, and shall straightway glorify him.
[33] Little children, yet a little while I am with you. Ye shall seek me: and as I said unto the Jews, Whither I go, ye cannot come; so now I say to you.
[34] A new commandment I give unto you, That ye love one another; as I have loved you, that ye also love one another.
[35] By this shall all men know that ye are my disciples, if ye have love one to another.
[36] Simon Peter said unto him, Lord, whither goest thou? Jesus answered him, Whither I go, thou canst not follow me now; but thou shalt follow me afterwards.
[37] Peter said unto him, Lord, why cannot I follow thee now? I will lay down my life for thy sake.
[38] Jesus answered him, Wilt thou lay down thy life for my sake? Verily, verily, I say unto thee, The cock shall not crow, till thou hast denied me thrice.

John 14

[1] Let not your heart be troubled: ye believe in God, believe also in me.
[2] In my Father's house are many mansions: if it were not so, I would have told you. I go to prepare a place for you.
[3] And if I go and prepare a place for you, I will come again, and receive you unto myself; that where I am, there ye may be also.
[4] And whither I go ye know, and the way ye know.
[5] Thomas saith unto him, Lord, we know not whither thou goest; and how can we know the way?

[6] Jesus saith unto him, I am the way, the truth, and the life: no man cometh unto the Father, but by me.

[7] If ye had known me, ye should have known my Father also: and from henceforth ye know him, and have seen him.

[8] Philip saith unto him, Lord, shew us the Father, and it sufficeth us.

[9] Jesus saith unto him, Have I been so long time with you, and yet hast thou not known me, Philip? he that hath seen me hath seen the Father; and how sayest thou then, Shew us the Father?

[10] Believest thou not that I am in the Father, and the Father in me? the words that I speak unto you I speak not of myself: but the Father that dwelleth in me, he doeth the works.

[11] Believe me that I am in the Father, and the Father in me: or else believe me for the very works' sake.

[12] Verily, verily, I say unto you, He that believeth on me, the works that I do shall he do also; and greater works than these shall he do; because I go unto my Father.

[13] And whatsoever ye shall ask in my name, that will I do, that the Father may be glorified in the Son.

[14] If ye shall ask any thing in my name, I will do it.

[15] If ye love me, keep my commandments.

[16] And I will pray the Father, and he shall give you another Comforter, that he may abide with you for ever;

[17] Even the Spirit of truth; whom the world cannot receive, because it seeth him not, neither knoweth him: but ye know him; for he dwelleth with you, and shall be in you.

[18] I will not leave you comfortless: I will come to you.

[19] Yet a little while, and the world seeth me no more; but ye see me: because I live, ye shall live also.

[20] At that day ye shall know that I am in my Father, and ye in me, and I in you.

[21] He that hath my commandments, and keepeth them, he it is that loveth me: and he that loveth me shall be loved of my Father, and I will love him, and will manifest myself to him.

[22] Judas saith unto him, not Iscariot, Lord, how is it that thou wilt manifest thyself unto us, and not unto the world?

[23] Jesus answered and said unto him, If a man love me, he will keep my words: and my Father will love him, and we will come unto him, and make our abode with him.

[24] He that loveth me not keepeth not my sayings: and the word which ye hear is not mine, but the Father's which sent me.

[25] These things have I spoken unto you, being yet present with you.

[26] But the Comforter, which is the Holy Ghost, whom the Father will send in my name, he shall teach you all things, and bring all things to your remembrance, whatsoever I have said unto you.

[27] Peace I leave with you, my peace I give unto you: not as the world giveth, give I unto you. Let not your heart be troubled, neither let it be afraid.

[28] Ye have heard how I said unto you, I go away, and come again unto you. If ye loved me, ye would rejoice, because I said, I go unto the Father: for my Father is greater than I.

[29] And now I have told you before it come to pass, that, when it is come to pass, ye might believe.

[30] Hereafter I will not talk much with you: for the prince of this world cometh, and hath nothing in me.

[31] But that the world may know that I love the Father; and as the Father gave me commandment, even so I do. Arise, let us go hence.

John 15

[1] I am the true vine, and my Father is the husbandman.

[2] Every branch in me that beareth not fruit he taketh away: and every branch that beareth fruit, he purgeth it, that it may bring forth more fruit.

[3] Now ye are clean through the word which I have spoken unto you.

[4] Abide in me, and I in you. As the branch cannot bear fruit of itself, except it abide in the vine; no more can ye, except ye abide in me.

[5] I am the vine, ye are the branches: He that abideth in me, and I in him, the same bringeth forth much fruit: for without me ye can do nothing.

[6] If a man abide not in me, he is cast forth as a branch, and is withered; and men gather them, and cast them into the fire, and they are burned.

[7] If ye abide in me, and my words abide in you, ye shall ask what ye will, and it shall be done unto you.

[8] Herein is my Father glorified, that ye bear much fruit; so shall ye be my disciples.

[9] As the Father hath loved me, so have I loved you: continue ye in my love.

[10] If ye keep my commandments, ye shall abide in my love; even as I have kept my Father's commandments, and abide in his love.

[11] These things have I spoken unto you, that my joy might remain in you, and that your joy might be full.

[12] This is my commandment, That ye love one another, as I have loved you.

[13] Greater love hath no man than this, that a man lay down his life for his friends.

[14] Ye are my friends, if ye do whatsoever I command you.

[15] Henceforth I call you not servants; for the servant knoweth not what his lord doeth: but I have called you friends; for all things that I have heard of my Father I have made known unto you.

[16] Ye have not chosen me, but I have chosen you, and ordained you, that ye should go and bring forth fruit, and that your fruit should remain: that whatsoever ye shall ask of the Father in my name, he may give it you.

[17] These things I command you, that ye love one another.

[18] If the world hate you, ye know that it hated me before it hated you.

[19] If ye were of the world, the world would love his own: but because ye are not of the world, but I have chosen you out of the world, therefore the world hateth you.

[20] Remember the word that I said unto you, The servant is not greater than his lord. If they have persecuted me, they will also

persecute you; if they have kept my saying, they will keep yours also.

[21] But all these things will they do unto you for my name's sake, because they know not him that sent me.

[22] If I had not come and spoken unto them, they had not had sin: but now they have no cloke for their sin.

[23] He that hateth me hateth my Father also.

[24] If I had not done among them the works which none other man did, they had not had sin: but now have they both seen and hated both me and my Father.

[25] But this cometh to pass, that the word might be fulfilled that is written in their law, They hated me without a cause.

[26] But when the Comforter is come, whom I will send unto you from the Father, even the Spirit of truth, which proceedeth from the Father, he shall testify of me:

[27] And ye also shall bear witness, because ye have been with me from the beginning.

John 16

[1] These things have I spoken unto you, that ye should not be offended.

[2] They shall put you out of the synagogues: yea, the time cometh, that whosoever killeth you will think that he doeth God service.

[3] And these things will they do unto you, because they have not known the Father, nor me.

[4] But these things have I told you, that when the time shall come, ye may remember that I told you of them. And these things I said not unto you at the beginning, because I was with you.

[5] But now I go my way to him that sent me; and none of you asketh me, Whither goest thou?

[6] But because I have said these things unto you, sorrow hath filled your heart.

[7] Nevertheless I tell you the truth; It is expedient for you that I go away: for if I go not away, the Comforter will not come unto you; but if I depart, I will send him unto you.

[8] And when he is come, he will reprove the world of sin, and of righteousness, and of judgment:

[9] Of sin, because they believe not on me;

[10] Of righteousness, because I go to my Father, and ye see me no more;

[11] Of judgment, because the prince of this world is judged.

[12] I have yet many things to say unto you, but ye cannot bear them now.

[13] Howbeit when he, the Spirit of truth, is come, he will guide you into all truth: for he shall not speak of himself; but whatsoever he shall hear, that shall he speak: and he will shew you things to come.

[14] He shall glorify me: for he shall receive of mine, and shall shew it unto you.

[15] All things that the Father hath are mine: therefore said I, that he shall take of mine, and shall shew it unto you.

[16] A little while, and ye shall not see me: and again, a little while, and ye shall see me, because I go to the Father.

[17] Then said some of his disciples among themselves, What is this that he saith unto us, A little while, and ye shall not see me: and again, a little while, and ye shall see me: and, Because I go to the Father?

[18] They said therefore, What is this that he saith, A little while? we cannot tell what he saith.

[19] Now Jesus knew that they were desirous to ask him, and said unto them, Do ye inquire among yourselves of that I said, A little while, and ye shall not see me: and again, a little while, and ye shall see me?

[20] Verily, verily, I say unto you, That ye shall weep and lament, but the world shall rejoice: and ye shall be sorrowful, but your sorrow shall be turned into joy.

[21] A woman when she is in travail hath sorrow, because her hour is come: but as soon as she is delivered of the child, she remembereth no more the anguish, for joy that a man is born into the world.

[22] And ye now therefore have sorrow: but I will see you again, and your heart shall rejoice, and your joy no man taketh from you.

[**23**] And in that day ye shall ask me nothing. Verily, verily, I say unto you, Whatsoever ye shall ask the Father in my name, he will give it you.

[**24**] Hitherto have ye asked nothing in my name: ask, and ye shall receive, that your joy may be full.

[**25**] These things have I spoken unto you in proverbs: but the time cometh, when I shall no more speak unto you in proverbs, but I shall shew you plainly of the Father.

[**26**] At that day ye shall ask in my name: and I say not unto you, that I will pray the Father for you:

[**27**] For the Father himself loveth you, because ye have loved me, and have believed that I came out from God.

[**28**] I came forth from the Father, and am come into the world: again, I leave the world, and go to the Father.

[**29**] His disciples said unto him, Lo, now speakest thou plainly, and speakest no proverb.

[**30**] Now are we sure that thou knowest all things, and needest not that any man should ask thee: by this we believe that thou camest forth from God.

[**31**] Jesus answered them, Do ye now believe?

[**32**] Behold, the hour cometh, yea, is now come, that ye shall be scattered, every man to his own, and shall leave me alone: and yet I am not alone, because the Father is with me.

[**33**] These things I have spoken unto you, that in me ye might have peace. In the world ye shall have tribulation: but be of good cheer; I have overcome the world.

John 17

[1] These words spake Jesus, and lifted up his eyes to heaven, and said, Father, the hour is come; glorify thy Son, that thy Son also may glorify thee:

[2] As thou hast given him power over all flesh, that he should give eternal life to as many as thou hast given him.

[3] And this is life eternal, that they might know thee the only true God, and Jesus Christ, whom thou hast sent.

[4] I have glorified thee on the earth: I have finished the work which thou gavest me to do.

[5] And now, O Father, glorify thou me with thine own self with the glory which I had with thee before the world was.

[6] I have manifested thy name unto the men which thou gavest me out of the world: thine they were, and thou gavest them me; and they have kept thy word.

[7] Now they have known that all things whatsoever thou hast given me are of thee.

[8] For I have given unto them the words which thou gavest me; and they have received them, and have known surely that I came out from thee, and they have believed that thou didst send me.

[9] I pray for them: I pray not for the world, but for them which thou hast given me; for they are thine.

[10] And all mine are thine, and thine are mine; and I am glorified in them.

[11] And now I am no more in the world, but these are in the world, and I come to thee. Holy Father, keep through thine own name those whom thou hast given me, that they may be one, as we are.

[12] While I was with them in the world, I kept them in thy name: those that thou gavest me I have kept, and none of them is lost, but the son of perdition; that the scripture might be fulfilled.

[13] And now come I to thee; and these things I speak in the world, that they might have my joy fulfilled in themselves.

[14] I have given them thy word; and the world hath hated them, because they are not of the world, even as I am not of the world.

[15] I pray not that thou shouldest take them out of the world, but that thou shouldest keep them from the evil.

[16] They are not of the world, even as I am not of the world.

[17] Sanctify them through thy truth: thy word is truth.

[18] As thou hast sent me into the world, even so have I also sent them into the world.

[19] And for their sakes I sanctify myself, that they also might be sanctified through the truth.

[20] Neither pray I for these alone, but for them also which shall believe on me through their word;

[21] That they all may be one; as thou, Father, art in me, and I in thee, that they also may be one in us: that the world may believe that thou hast sent me.

[22] And the glory which thou gavest me I have given them; that they may be one, even as we are one:

[23] I in them, and thou in me, that they may be made perfect in one; and that the world may know that thou hast sent me, and hast loved them, as thou hast loved me.

[24] Father, I will that they also, whom thou hast given me, be with me where I am; that they may behold my glory, which thou hast given me: for thou lovedst me before the foundation of the world.

[25] O righteous Father, the world hath not known thee: but I have known thee, and these have known that thou hast sent me.

[26] And I have declared unto them thy name, and will declare it: that the love wherewith thou hast loved me may be in them, and I in them.

John 18

[1] When Jesus had spoken these words, he went forth with his disciples over the brook Cedron, where was a garden, into the which he entered, and his disciples.

[2] And Judas also, which betrayed him, knew the place: for Jesus ofttimes resorted thither with his disciples.

[3] Judas then, having received a band of men and officers from the chief priests and Pharisees, cometh thither with lanterns and torches and weapons.

[4] Jesus therefore, knowing all things that should come upon him, went forth, and said unto them, Whom seek ye?

[5] They answered him, Jesus of Nazareth. Jesus saith unto them, I am he. And Judas also, which betrayed him, stood with them.

[6] As soon then as he had said unto them, I am he, they went backward, and fell to the ground.

[7] Then asked he them again, Whom seek ye? And they said, Jesus of Nazareth.

[8] Jesus answered, I have told you that I am he: if therefore ye seek me, let these go their way:

[9] That the saying might be fulfilled, which he spake, Of them which thou gavest me have I lost none.

[10] Then Simon Peter having a sword drew it, and smote the high priest's servant, and cut off his right ear. The servant's name was Malchus.

[11] Then said Jesus unto Peter, Put up thy sword into the sheath: the cup which my Father hath given me, shall I not drink it?

[12] Then the band and the captain and officers of the Jews took Jesus, and bound him,

[13] And led him away to Annas first; for he was father in law to Caiaphas, which was the high priest that same year.

[14] Now Caiaphas was he, which gave counsel to the Jews, that it was expedient that one man should die for the people.

[15] And Simon Peter followed Jesus, and so did another disciple: that disciple was known unto the high priest, and went in with Jesus into the palace of the high priest.

[16] But Peter stood at the door without. Then went out that other disciple, which was known unto the high priest, and spake unto her that kept the door, and brought in Peter.

[17] Then saith the damsel that kept the door unto Peter, Art not thou also one of this man's disciples? He saith, I am not.

[18] And the servants and officers stood there, who had made a fire of coals; for it was cold: and they warmed themselves: and Peter stood with them, and warmed himself.

[19] The high priest then asked Jesus of his disciples, and of his doctrine.

[20] Jesus answered him, I spake openly to the world; I ever taught in the synagogue, and in the temple, whither the Jews always resort; and in secret have I said nothing.

[21] Why askest thou me? ask them which heard me, what I have said unto them: behold, they know what I said.

[22] And when he had thus spoken, one of the officers which stood by struck Jesus with the palm of his hand, saying, Answerest thou the high priest so?

[**23**] Jesus answered him, If I have spoken evil, bear witness of the evil: but if well, why smitest thou me?

[**24**] Now Annas had sent him bound unto Caiaphas the high priest.

[**25**] And Simon Peter stood and warmed himself. They said therefore unto him, Art not thou also one of his disciples? He denied it, and said, I am not.

[**26**] One of the servants of the high priest, being his kinsman whose ear Peter cut off, saith, Did not I see thee in the garden with him?

[**27**] Peter then denied again: and immediately the cock crew.

[**28**] Then led they Jesus from Caiaphas unto the hall of judgment: and it was early; and they themselves went not into the judgment hall, lest they should be defiled; but that they might eat the passover.

[**29**] Pilate then went out unto them, and said, What accusation bring ye against this man?

[**30**] They answered and said unto him, If he were not a malefactor, we would not have delivered him up unto thee.

[**31**] Then said Pilate unto them, Take ye him, and judge him according to your law. The Jews therefore said unto him, It is not lawful for us to put any man to death:

[**32**] That the saying of Jesus might be fulfilled, which he spake, signifying what death he should die.

[**33**] Then Pilate entered into the judgment hall again, and called Jesus, and said unto him, Art thou the King of the Jews?

[**34**] Jesus answered him, Sayest thou this thing of thyself, or did others tell it thee of me?

[**35**] Pilate answered, Am I a Jew? Thine own nation and the chief priests have delivered thee unto me: what hast thou done?

[**36**] Jesus answered, My kingdom is not of this world: if my kingdom were of this world, then would my servants fight, that I should not be delivered to the Jews: but now is my kingdom not from hence.

[**37**] Pilate therefore said unto him, Art thou a king then? Jesus answered, Thou sayest that I am a king. To this end was I born, and for this cause came I into the world, that I should bear witness unto the truth. Every one that is of the truth heareth my voice.

[38] Pilate saith unto him, What is truth? And when he had said this, he went out again unto the Jews, and saith unto them, I find in him no fault at all.

[39] But ye have a custom, that I should release unto you one at the passover: will ye therefore that I release unto you the King of the Jews?

[40] Then cried they all again, saying, Not this man, but Barabbas. Now Barabbas was a robber.

John 19

[1] Then Pilate therefore took Jesus, and scourged him.

[2] And the soldiers platted a crown of thorns, and put it on his head, and they put on him a purple robe,

[3] And said, Hail, King of the Jews! and they smote him with their hands.

[4] Pilate therefore went forth again, and saith unto them, Behold, I bring him forth to you, that ye may know that I find no fault in him.

[5] Then came Jesus forth, wearing the crown of thorns, and the purple robe. And Pilate saith unto them, Behold the man!

[6] When the chief priests therefore and officers saw him, they cried out, saying, Crucify him, crucify him. Pilate saith unto them, Take ye him, and crucify him: for I find no fault in him.

[7] The Jews answered him, We have a law, and by our law he ought to die, because he made himself the Son of God.

[8] When Pilate therefore heard that saying, he was the more afraid;

[9] And went again into the judgment hall, and saith unto Jesus, Whence art thou? But Jesus gave him no answer.

[10] Then saith Pilate unto him, Speakest thou not unto me? knowest thou not that I have power to crucify thee, and have power to release thee?

[11] Jesus answered, Thou couldest have no power at all against me, except it were given thee from above: therefore he that delivered me unto thee hath the greater sin.

[12] And from thenceforth Pilate sought to release him: but the Jews cried out, saying, If thou let this man go, thou art not Caesar's friend: whosoever maketh himself a king speaketh against Caesar.

[13] When Pilate therefore heard that saying, he brought Jesus forth, and sat down in the judgment seat in a place that is called the Pavement, but in the Hebrew, Gabbatha.

[14] And it was the preparation of the passover, and about the sixth hour: and he saith unto the Jews, Behold your King!

[15] But they cried out, Away with him, away with him, crucify him. Pilate saith unto them, Shall I crucify your King? The chief priest answered, We have no king but Caesar.

[16] Then delivered he him therefore unto them to be crucified. And they took Jesus, and led him away.

[17] And he bearing his cross went forth into a place called the place of a skull, which is called in the Hebrew Golgotha:

[18] Where they crucified him, and two other with him, on either side one, and Jesus in the midst.

[19] And Pilate wrote a title, and put it on the cross. And the writing was, JESUS OF NAZARETH THE KING OF THE JEWS.

[20] This title then read many of the Jews: for the place where Jesus was crucified was nigh to the city: and it was written in Hebrew, and Greek, and Latin.

[21] Then said the chief priests of the Jews to Pilate, Write not, The King of the Jews; but that he said, I am King of the Jews.

[22] Pilate answered, What I have written I have written.

[23] Then the soldiers, when they had crucified Jesus, took his garments, and made four parts, to every soldier a part; and also his coat: now the coat was without seam, woven from the top throughout.

[24] They said therefore among themselves, Let us not rend it, but cast lots for it, whose it shall be: that the scripture might be fulfilled, which saith, They parted my raiment among them, and for my vesture they did cast lots. These things therefore the soldiers did.

[25] Now there stood by the cross of Jesus his mother, and his mother's sister, Mary the wife of Cleophas, and Mary Magdalene.

[26] When Jesus therefore saw his mother, and the disciple standing by, whom he loved, he saith unto his mother, Woman, behold thy son!

[27] Then saith he to the disciple, Behold thy mother! And from that hour that disciple took her unto his own home.

[28] After this, Jesus knowing that all things were now accomplished, that the scripture might be fulfilled, saith, I thirst.

[29] Now there was set a vessel full of vinegar: and they filled a spunge with vinegar, and put it upon hyssop, and put it to his mouth.

[30] When Jesus therefore had received the vinegar, he said, It is finished: and he bowed his head, and gave up the ghost.

[31] The Jews therefore, because it was the preparation, that the bodies should not remain upon the cross on the sabbath day, (for that sabbath day was an high day,) besought Pilate that their legs might be broken, and that they might be taken away.

[32] Then came the soldiers, and brake the legs of the first, and of the other which was crucified with him.

[33] But when they came to Jesus, and saw that he was dead already, they brake not his legs:

[34] But one of the soldiers with a spear pierced his side, and forthwith came there out blood and water.

[35] And he that saw it bare record, and his record is true: and he knoweth that he saith true, that ye might believe.

[36] For these things were done, that the scripture should be fulfilled, A bone of him shall not be broken.

[37] And again another scripture saith, They shall look on him whom they pierced.

[38] And after this Joseph of Arimathaea, being a disciple of Jesus, but secretly for fear of the Jews, besought Pilate that he might take away the body of Jesus: and Pilate gave him leave. He came therefore, and took the body of Jesus.

[39] And there came also Nicodemus, which at the first came to Jesus by night, and brought a mixture of myrrh and aloes, about an hundred pound weight.

[40] Then took they the body of Jesus, and wound it in linen clothes

with the spices, as the manner of the Jews is to bury.

[41] Now in the place where he was crucified there was a garden; and in the garden a new sepulchre, wherein was never man yet laid.

[42] There laid they Jesus therefore because of the Jews' preparation day; for the sepulchre was nigh at hand.

John 20

[1] The first day of the week cometh Mary Magdalene early, when it was yet dark, unto the sepulchre, and seeth the stone taken away from the sepulchre.

[2] Then she runneth, and cometh to Simon Peter, and to the other disciple, whom Jesus loved, and saith unto them, They have taken away the Lord out of the sepulchre, and we know not where they have laid him.

[3] Peter therefore went forth, and that other disciple, and came to the sepulchre.

[4] So they ran both together: and the other disciple did outrun Peter, and came first to the sepulchre.

[5] And he stooping down, and looking in, saw the linen clothes lying; yet went he not in.

[6] Then cometh Simon Peter following him, and went into the sepulchre, and seeth the linen clothes lie,

[7] And the napkin, that was about his head, not lying with the linen clothes, but wrapped together in a place by itself.

[8] Then went in also that other disciple, which came first to the sepulchre, and he saw, and believed.

[9] For as yet they knew not the scripture, that he must rise again from the dead.

[10] Then the disciples went away again unto their own home.

[11] But Mary stood without at the sepulchre weeping: and as she wept, she stooped down, and looked into the sepulchre,

[12] And seeth two angels in white sitting, the one at the head, and the other at the feet, where the body of Jesus had lain.

[13] And they say unto her, Woman, why weepest thou? She saith unto them, Because they have taken away my Lord, and I know not where they have laid him.

[14] And when she had thus said, she turned herself back, and saw Jesus standing, and knew not that it was Jesus.

[15] Jesus saith unto her, Woman, why weepest thou? whom seekest thou? She, supposing him to be the gardener, saith unto him, Sir, if thou have borne him hence, tell me where thou hast laid him, and I will take him away.

[16] Jesus saith unto her, Mary. She turned herself, and saith unto him, Rabboni; which is to say, Master.

[17] Jesus saith unto her, Touch me not; for I am not yet ascended to my Father: but go to my brethren, and say unto them, I ascend unto my Father, and your Father; and to my God, and your God.

[18] Mary Magdalene came and told the disciples that she had seen the Lord, and that he had spoken these things unto her.

[19] Then the same day at evening, being the first day of the week, when the doors were shut where the disciples were assembled for fear of the Jews, came Jesus and stood in the midst, and saith unto them, Peace be unto you.

[20] And when he had so said, he shewed unto them his hands and his side. Then were the disciples glad, when they saw the Lord.

[21] Then said Jesus to them again, Peace be unto you: as my Father hath sent me, even so send I you.

[22] And when he had said this, he breathed on them, and saith unto them, Receive ye the Holy Ghost:

[23] Whose soever sins ye remit, they are remitted unto them; and whose soever sins ye retain, they are retained.

[24] But Thomas, one of the twelve, called Didymus, was not with them when Jesus came.

[25] The other disciples therefore said unto him, We have seen the Lord. But he said unto them, Except I shall see in his hands the print of the nails, and put my finger into the print of the nails, and thrust my hand into his side, I will not believe.

[26] And after eight days again his disciples were within, and Thomas with them: then came Jesus, the doors being shut, and

stood in the midst, and said, Peace be unto you.

[27] Then saith he to Thomas, reach hither thy finger, and behold my hands; and reach hither thy hand, and thrust it into my side: and be not faithless, but believing.

[28] And Thomas answered and said unto him, My Lord and my God.

[29] Jesus saith unto him, Thomas, because thou hast seen me, thou hast believed: blessed are they that have not seen, and yet have believed.

[30] And many other signs truly did Jesus in the presence of his disciples, which are not written in this book:

[31] But these are written, that ye might believe that Jesus is the Christ, the Son of God; and that believing ye might have life through his name.

John 21

[1] After these things Jesus shewed himself again to the disciples at the sea of Tiberias; and on this wise shewed he himself.

[2] There were together Simon Peter, and Thomas called Didymus, and Nathanael of Cana in Galilee, and the sons of Zebedee, and two other of his disciples.

[3] Simon Peter saith unto them, I go a fishing. They say unto him, We also go with thee. They went forth, and entered into a ship immediately; and that night they caught nothing.

[4] But when the morning was now come, Jesus stood on the shore: but the disciples knew not that it was Jesus.

[5] Then Jesus saith unto them, Children, have ye any meat? They answered him, No.

[6] And he said unto them, Cast the net on the right side of the ship, and ye shall find. They cast therefore, and now they were not able to draw it for the multitude of fishes.

[7] Therefore that disciple whom Jesus loved saith unto Peter, It is the Lord. Now when Simon Peter heard that it was the Lord, he girt his fisher's coat unto him, (for he was naked,) and did cast himself into the sea.

---

[8] And the other disciples came in a little ship; (for they were not far from land, but as it were two hundred cubits,) dragging the net with fishes.

[9] As soon then as they were come to land, they saw a fire of coals there, and fish laid thereon, and bread.

[10] Jesus saith unto them, Bring of the fish which ye have now caught.

[11] Simon Peter went up, and drew the net to land full of great fishes, and hundred and fifty and three: and for all there were so many, yet was not the net broken.

[12] Jesus saith unto them, Come and dine. And none of the disciples durst ask him, Who art thou? knowing that it was the Lord.

[13] Jesus then cometh, and taketh bread, and giveth them, and fish likewise.

[14] This is now the third time that Jesus shewed himself to his disciples, after that he was risen from the dead.

[15] So when they had dined, Jesus saith to Simon Peter, Simon, son of Jonas, lovest thou me more than these? He saith unto him, Yea, Lord; thou knowest that I love thee. He saith unto him, Feed my lambs.

[16] He saith to him again the second time, Simon, son of Jonas, lovest thou me? He saith unto him, Yea, Lord; thou knowest that I love thee. He saith unto him, Feed my sheep.

[17] He saith unto him the third time, Simon, son of Jonas, lovest thou me? Peter was grieved because he said unto him the third time, Lovest thou me? And he said unto him, Lord, thou knowest all things; thou knowest that I love thee. Jesus saith unto him, Feed my sheep.

[18] Verily, verily, I say unto thee, When thou wast young, thou girdedst thyself, and walkedst whither thou wouldest: but when thou shalt be old, thou shalt stretch forth thy hands, and another shall gird thee, and carry thee whither thou wouldest not.

[19] This spake he, signifying by what death he should glorify God. And when he had spoken this, he saith unto him, Follow me.

[20] Then Peter, turning about, seeth the disciple whom Jesus loved following; which also leaned on his breast at supper, and said, Lord,

which is he that betrayeth thee?

[**21**] Peter seeing him saith to Jesus, Lord, and what shall this man do?

[**22**] Jesus saith unto him, If I will that he tarry till I come, what is that to thee? follow thou me.

[**23**] Then went this saying abroad among the brethren, that that disciple should not die: yet Jesus said not unto him, He shall not die; but, If I will that he tarry till I come, what is that to thee?

[**24**] This is the disciple which testifieth of these things, and wrote these things: and we know that his testimony is true.

[**25**] And there are also many other things which Jesus did, the which, if they should be written every one, I suppose that even the world itself could not contain the books that should be written. Amen.

~~~~~~~~~~

"Ye are my friends, if ye do whatsoever I command you. Henceforth
I call you not servants; for the servant knoweth not what his lord doeth:
but I have called you friends;
for all things that I have heard of my Father I have made known unto you.
Ye have not chosen me, but I have chosen you, and ordained you,
that ye should go and bring forth fruit, and that your fruit should remain:
that whatsoever ye shall ask of the Father in my name, he may give it you."
~~~ John 15:14-15

Conclusion
Let Us Hear the Conclusion

~ ~ ~ ~ ~

"Let us hear the conclusion of the whole matter:
Fear God, and keep his commandments:
for this is the whole duty of man."
~~~ Ecclesiastes 12:13

~ ~ ~ ~ ~

So here we are, at the conclusion of this book, a simple walk, if you will. But the great journey lay ahead. A journey of discovery and abundance, for as Jesus said, *"I am come that they might have life, and that they might have it more abundantly."*[154] Know in your heart He was talking about you!

You and I were born for a time such as this! A time of great responsibility to be greatly borne, a time when we renew our faith and our hope, and embrace the promises of God. A time of dedicating or rededicating to studying and meditating on the Word of God, so we might have a more personal and intimate relationship with Him. A time when we might fully realize God's personal plan for our particular lives, and we might carry the banner of the great crusade.

King Solomon, arguably the wisest man of the Old Testament, gave us the benefit of his lifelong journey, a life of trial and triumph, studying and meditating on Holy Scripture, a life of learning and walking with God. Solomon gave us the benefit of what he ultimately learned in his lifelong journey, and he shares it with us in

---

[154] John 10:10.

Ecclesiastes 12:13, *"Let us hear the conclusion of the whole matter: Fear God, and keep his commandments: for this is the whole duty of man."*

Last Christmas, during a hike with our dogs in the local state park, my wife, Denise, asked me why I was writing this book. I replied I was following the Great Commission.[155] Whatever gifts God has given me belong to Him, and it is my ongoing desire to spread the Good News and seek His will in all that I do. This is why I was born.

Always remember, you and I are commissioned by God. It is a good and noble Quest. In Mark 16:15, we read His last great commandment:

> And He said unto them, Go ye into all the world, and preach the gospel to every creature.

Let it be said of us that we mastered our moment, that we held tight to the reigns of our destiny, that we were good and faithful, and we refused to settle for anything less than what our God-given talents could achieve. Surrender to the Lord and live a godly life, for this is the whole duty of man.

Amen.

~~~~~~~~~~

"In the beginning was the Word,
and the Word was with God, and the Word was God."
~~~ John 1:1

---

[155] Mark 16:15.

Profitable Passages for
Instruction in Righteousness

~ ~ ~ ~ ~

"So shall my word be that goeth forth out of my mouth:
it shall not return unto me void, but it shall accomplish that which I please,
and it shall prosper in the thing whereto I sent it."
~~~ Isaiah 55:11

~ ~ ~ ~ ~

2 Timothy 3:16-17 states, *"[16]All scripture is given by inspiration of God, and is profitable for doctrine, for reproof, for correction, for instruction in righteousness: [17]That the man of God may be perfect, thoroughly furnished unto all good works."* Know with all of your heart, and soul, and mind, this was written for you! You are special to God. Yes, the God who created the universe and made all things is personally interested in you and your future. Here is what God says: *"'For I know the plans that I have for you,' declares the Lord, 'plans for welfare and not for calamity to give you a future and a hope.'"*[156] He gave you and me the Word so that we might have a restored close and personal relationship with Him. He loves you! Believe in Him, and trust Him! His Word applies to you!

With this in mind, the remainder of this work is dedicated to heralding the Word of God, as it is given from the mouth of God. It will not return void. It will accomplish what God wants. It will prosper you!

Whether you are afflicted with loneliness, poverty, grief, or just have questions about God and His plans for you, the following

---

[156] Jeremiah 29:11, NASB.

passages gleamed from Holy Scripture are proffered for your edification. They are not all-inclusive. They are but a glimpse into the Word of God on these topics. You are encouraged to read the Holy Bible every day, and walk in the light of His truth for godly living.

Do not fall for the naysayers who seek to discourage you. They say, *"The Bible is too difficult to read."* It is not! Rely on the promises of God in Matthew 7:7-8, *"[7]Ask and it will be given to you; seek and you will find; knock and the door will be opened to you. [8]For everyone who asks receives; the one who seeks finds; and to the one who knocks, the door will be opened."* Count on Him in the person of the Holy Spirit to guide you through Scripture, and to a closer, personal relationship with Him. This is the path to living a godly life!

Seize this moment! Discover personal growth and the way to a successful life! James 4:8 promises, *"Draw nigh to God, and he will draw nigh to you."* Draw near to God!

~~~~~~~~~~

"For thou art my rock and my fortress;
therefore for thy name's sake lead me, and guide me."
~~~ Psalm 31:3

Passages On
God

~ ~ ~ ~ ~

"In the beginning God created the heaven and the earth."
~~~ Genesis 1:1

"In the beginning was the Word,
and the Word was with God, and the Word was God."
~~~ John 1:1

"I am Alpha and Omega, the beginning and the ending, saith the
Lord, which is, and which was, and which is to come, the Almighty."
~~~ Revelation 1:18

"Thy word is a lamp unto my feet, and a light unto my path."
~~~ Psalm 119:105

"Herein is love, not that we loved God, but that he loved us, and
sent his Son to be the propitiation for our sins."
~~~ 1 John 4:10

"God is love;
and he that dwelleth in love dwelleth in God, and God in him."
~~~ 1 John 4:16

"For unto you is born this day in the city of David a Saviour,
which is Christ the Lord."
~~~ Luke 2:11

"In whose hand is the soul of every living thing,
and the breath of all mankind."
~~~ Job 12:10

"For God so loved the world, that he gave his only begotten Son,
that whosoever believeth in him should not perish,
but have everlasting life."
~~~ John 3:16

"Then spake Jesus again unto them, saying, I am the light of the
world: he that followeth me shall not walk in darkness,
but shall have the light of life."
~~~ John 8:12

"But Jesus beheld them, and said unto them,
With men this is impossible;
but with God all things are possible."
~~~Matthew 19:26

"The LORD on high is mightier than the noise of many waters, yea,
than the mighty waves of the sea."
~~~ Psalm 93:4

"He telleth the number of the stars;
he calleth them all by their names."
~~~ Psalm 147:4

"For there are three that bear record in heaven, the Father, the
Word, and the Holy Ghost: and these three are one."
~~~ 1 John 5:7

"Jesus saith unto him, I am the way, the truth, and the life: no man
cometh unto the Father, but by me."
~~~ John 14:6

"And I heard as it were the voice of a great multitude, and as the
voice of many waters, and as the voice of mighty thunderings,
saying, Alleluia: for the Lord God omnipotent reigneth."
~~~ Revelation 19:6

"I Jesus have sent mine angel to testify unto you these things in the churches. I am the root and the offspring of David, and the bright and morning star."
~~~ Revelation 22:16

~~~~~~~~~~~

These passages are but a glimpse into the Word of God on this subject. You are encouraged to read the Holy Bible every day, and walk in the light of His truth for godly living.

Passages On
You

~ ~ ~ ~ ~

"For God so loved the world, that he gave his only begotten Son,
that whosoever believeth in him should not perish,
but have everlasting life."
~~~ John 3:16

"Whether therefore ye eat, or drink, or whatsoever ye do,
do all to the glory of God."
~~~ Psalm 37:23

"But my God shall supply all your need
According to his riches in glory by Christ Jesus."
~~~ Philippians 4:19

"Ye are the light of the world.
A city that is set on an hill cannot be hid.
Neither do men light a candle,
and put it under a bushel, but on a candlestick;
and it giveth light unto all that are in the house.
Let your light so shine before men, that they may see your good
works, and glorify your Father which is in heaven."
~~~ Matthew 5:14-16

"But the very hairs of your head are all numbered.
Fear ye not therefore, ye are of more value than many sparrows."
~~~ Matthew 10:30-31

"Before I formed thee in the belly I knew thee;
and before thou camest forth out of the womb I sanctified thee,
and I ordained thee a prophet unto the nations."
~~~ Jeremiah 1:5

"Take fast hold of instruction; let her not go:
keep her; for she is thy life."
~~~ Proverbs 4:13

"Hear counsel, and receive instruction,
that thou mayest be wise in thy latter end."
~~~ Proverbs 19:20

"But we are bound to give thanks alway to God for you,
brethren beloved of the Lord, because God hath from the beginning
chosen you to salvation through sanctification of the Spirit
and belief of the truth:
Whereunto he called you by our gospel,
to the obtaining of the glory of our Lord Jesus Christ.
Therefore, brethren, stand fast, and hold the traditions
which ye have been taught, whether by word, or our epistle."
~~~ 2 Thessalonians 2:13-15

"Let us hear the conclusion of the whole matter:
Fear God, and keep his commandments:
for this is the whole duty of man."
~~~ Ecclesiastes 12:13

~~~~~~~~~~~

*These passages are but a glimpse into the Word of God on this subject.
You are encouraged to read the Holy Bible every day,
and walk in the light of His truth for godly living.*

Passages On
Wisdom

~ ~ ~ ~ ~

"For where envying and strife is,
there is confusion and every evil work.
But the wisdom that is from above is first pure, then peaceable,
gentle, and easy to be intreated, full of mercy and good fruits,
without partiality, and without hypocrisy."
~~~ James 3:16-17

"The fear of the LORD is the beginning of wisdom: and the
knowledge of the holy is understanding."
~~~ Proverbs 9:10

"Wise men lay up knowledge:
but the mouth of the foolish is near destruction."
~~~ Proverbs 10:14

"So shall the knowledge of wisdom be unto thy soul:
when thou hast found it, then there shall be a reward,
and thy expectation shall not be cut off."
~~~ Proverbs 24:14

"But we speak the wisdom of God in a mystery, even the hidden
wisdom, which God ordained before the world unto our glory:
Which none of the princes of this world knew:
for had they known it, they would
not have crucified the Lord of glory.
But as it is written, Eye hath not seen, nor ear heard,
neither have entered into the heart of man,
the things which God hath prepared for them that love him."
~~~ 1 Corinthians 2:7-9

"Happy is the man that findeth wisdom,
and the man that getteth understanding.
For the merchandise of it is better than the merchandise of silver,
and the gain thereof than fine gold."
~~~ Proverbs 3:13-14

"Buy the truth, and sell it not;
also wisdom, and instruction, and understanding."
~~~ Proverbs 23:23

"For wisdom is a defence, and money is a defence:
but the excellency of knowledge is,
that wisdom giveth life to them that have it."
~~~ Ecclesiastes 7:12

"Wisdom strengtheneth the wise more than ten mighty men
which are in the city."
~~~ Ecclesiastes 7:19

"For whoso findeth me [Wisdom] findeth life,
and shall obtain favour of the LORD.
But he that sinneth against me wrongeth his own soul:
all they that hate me love death."
~~~ Proverbs 8:35-36

~~~~~~~~~~

These passages are but a glimpse into the Word of God on this subject.
You are encouraged to read the Holy Bible every day,
and walk in the light of His truth for godly living.

Passages On
Avoiding Evil

~ ~ ~ ~ ~

"By mercy and truth iniquity is purged:
and by the fear of the LORD men depart from evil."
~~~ Proverbs 16:6

"Beloved, follow not that which is evil, but that which is good.
He that doeth good is of God:
but he that doeth evil hath not seen God."
~~~ 3 John 1:11

"As obedient children, not fashioning yourselves
according to the former lusts in your ignorance:
But as he which hath called you is holy,
so be ye holy in all manner of conversation;
Because it is written, Be ye holy; for I am holy."
~~~ 1 Peter 1:14-16

"Pray without ceasing.
In every thing give thanks:
for this is the will of God in Christ Jesus concerning you.
Quench not the Spirit.
Despise not prophesyings.
Prove all things; hold fast that which is good.
Abstain from all appearance of evil.
And the very God of peace sanctify you wholly;
and I pray God your whole spirit and soul and body be preserved
blameless unto the coming of our Lord Jesus Christ.
Faithful is he that calleth you, who also will do it."
~~~ 1 Thessalonians 5:17-24

"Deliver me, O my God, out of the hand of the wicked,
out of the hand of the unrighteous and cruel man."
~~~ Psalm 71:4

"Keep me from the snares which they have laid for me,
and the gins of the workers of iniquity."
~~~ Psalm 141:9

"Let love be without dissimulation.
Abhor that which is evil; cleave to that which is good."
~~~ Romans 12:9

"Be not overcome of evil, but overcome evil with good."
~~~ Romans 12:21

~~~~~~~~~~

These passages are but a glimpse into the Word of God on this subject.
You are encouraged to read the Holy Bible every day,
and walk in the light of His truth for godly living.

Passages On
Communication

~ ~ ~ ~ ~

"Let the words of my mouth, and the meditation of my heart, be acceptable in thy sight, O LORD, my strength, and my redeemer."
~~~ Psalm 19:14

"If any man speak, let him speak as the oracles of God; if any man minister, let him do it as of the ability which God giveth:
that God in all things may be glorified through Jesus Christ,
to whom be praise and dominion for ever and ever."
~~~ 1 Peter 4:6

"Be not deceived: evil communications corrupt good manners."
~~~ 1 Corinthians 15:33

"Blessings are upon the head of the just: but violence covereth the mouth of the wicked."
~~~ Proverbs 10:6

"The mouth of a righteous man is a well of life: but violence covereth the mouth of the wicked.
Hatred stirreth up strifes: but love covereth all sins."
~~~ Proverbs 10:11-12

"The words of the wicked are to lie in wait for blood:
but the mouth of the upright shall deliver them."
~~~ Proverbs 12:6

"A man shall be satisfied with good by the fruit of his mouth: and the recompence of a man's hands shall be rendered unto him."
~~~ Proverbs 12:14

"There is that speaketh like the piercings of a sword:
but the tongue of the wise is health."
~~~ Proverbs 12:18

"He that keepeth his mouth keepeth his life:
but he that openeth wide his lips shall have destruction."
~~~ Proverbs 13:3

"The heart of the righteous studieth to answer:
but the mouth of the wicked poureth out evil things."
~~~ Proverbs 15:28

"Even a fool, when he holdeth his peace, is counted wise:
and he that shutteth his lips is esteemed a man of understanding."
~~~ Proverbs 17:28

"A man's belly shall be satisfied with the fruit of his mouth;
and with the increase of his lips shall he be filled.
Death and life are in the power of the tongue:
and they that love it shall eat the fruit thereof."
~~~ Proverbs 18:20-21

"Whoso keepeth his mouth and his tongue
keepeth his soul from troubles."
~~~ Proverbs 21:23

"Seest thou a man that is hasty in his words?
there is more hope of a fool than of him."
~~~ Proverbs 29:20

"Set a watch, O LORD, before my mouth; keep the door of my lips."
~~~ Psalm 141:3

"For by thy words thou shalt be justified,
and by thy words thou shalt be condemned."
~~~ Matthew 12:37

"Thou hast proved mine heart; thou hast visited me in the night;
thou hast tried me, and shalt find nothing;
I am purposed that my mouth shall not transgress."
~~~ Psalm 17:3

"The LORD's voice crieth unto the city, and the man of wisdom shall
see thy name: hear ye the rod, and who hath appointed it."
~~~ Micah 6:9

~~~~~~~~~~~

*These passages are but a glimpse into the Word of God on this subject.
You are encouraged to read the Holy Bible every day,
and walk in the light of His truth for godly living.*

Passages On
Mercy & Forgiveness

~ ~ ~ ~ ~

"As far as the east is from the west,
so far hath he removed our transgressions from us."
~~~ Psalm 103:12

"To the Lord our God belong mercies and forgivenesses,
though we have rebelled against him;
Neither have we obeyed the voice of the LORD our God,
to walk in his laws,
which he set before us by his servants the prophets."
~~~ Daniel 9:9-10

"Blessed are the merciful: for they shall obtain mercy."
~~~ Matthew 5:7

"And forgive us our debts, as we forgive our debtors."
~~~ Matthew 6:12

"Then came Peter to him, and said, Lord, how oft shall my brother
sin against me, and I forgive him? till seven times?
Jesus saith unto him, I say not unto thee, Until seven times:
but, Until seventy times seven."
~~~ Matthew 18:21-22

"Be ye therefore merciful, as your Father also is merciful.
Judge not, and ye shall not be judged: condemn not, and ye shall
not be condemned: forgive, and ye shall be forgiven:
Give, and it shall be given unto you; good measure, pressed down,
and shaken together, and running over,

shall men give into your bosom. For with the same measure
that ye mete withal it shall be measured to you again."
~~~ Luke 6:36-38

"And if he trespass against thee seven times in a day,
and seven times in a day turn again to thee, saying, I repent;
thou shalt forgive him."
~~~ Luke 17:4

"He hath shewed thee, O man, what is good; and what doth the
LORD require of thee, but to do justly, and to love mercy,
and to walk humbly with thy God?"
~~~ Micah 6:8

"And be ye kind one to another, tenderhearted, forgiving one
another, even as God for Christ's sake hath forgiven you."
~~~ Ephesians 4:32

"Forbearing one another, and forgiving one another,
if any man have a quarrel against any:
even as Christ forgave you, so also do ye."
~~~ Colossians 3:13

"Knowing this, that our old man is crucified with him,
that the body of sin might be destroyed, that henceforth we should
not serve sin. For he that is dead is freed from sin."
~~~ Romans 6:6-7

"There is therefore now no condemnation to them which are in
Christ Jesus, who walk not after the flesh, but after the Spirit.
For the law of the Spirit of life in Christ Jesus hath made me
free from the law of sin and death."
~~~ Romans 8:1-2

"Whereof the Holy Ghost also is a witness to us:
for after that he had said before,
This is the covenant that I will make with them after those days,
saith the Lord, I will put my laws into their hearts,
and in their minds will I write them;
And their sins and iniquities will I remember no more."
~~~ Hebrews 10:15-17

~~~~~~~~~~

These passages are but a glimpse into the Word of God on this subject.
You are encouraged to read the Holy Bible every day,
and walk in the light of His truth for godly living.

Passages On
Children

~ ~ ~ ~ ~

"Honour thy father and thy mother: that thy days may be long upon the land which the LORD thy God giveth thee."
~~~ Exodus 20:12

"Honour thy father and thy mother, as the Lord thy God hath commanded thee; that thy days may be prolonged, and that it may go well with thee, in the land which the Lord thy God giveth thee."
~~~ Deuteronomy 5:16

"Children, obey your parents in all things: for this is well pleasing unto the Lord."
~~~ Colossians 3:20

"My son, if sinners entice thee, consent thou not."
~~~ Proverbs 1:10

"Take fast hold of instruction; let her not go: keep her; for she is thy life."
~~~ Proverbs 4:13

"He that walketh with wise men shall be wise: but a companion of fools shall be destroyed."
~~~ Proverbs 13:10

"Hear counsel, and receive instruction, that thou mayest be wise in thy latter end."
~~~ Proverbs 19:20

"Whosoever therefore shall humble himself as this little child,
the same is greatest in the kingdom of heaven.
And whoso shall receive one such little child
in my name receiveth me."
~~~ Matthew 18:4-5

"The LORD by wisdom hath founded the earth;
by understanding hath he established the heavens.
By his knowledge the depths are broken up,
and the clouds drop down the dew.
My son, let not them depart from thine eyes:
keep sound wisdom and discretion:
So shall they be life unto thy soul, and grace to thy neck.
Then shalt thou walk in thy way safely,
and thy foot shall not stumble.
When thou liest down, thou shalt not be afraid:
yea, thou shalt lie down, and thy sleep shall be sweet."
~~~ Proverbs 3:19-24

"And they brought young children to him, that he should touch
them: and his disciples rebuked those that brought them.
But when Jesus saw it, he was much displeased,
and said unto them,
Suffer the little children to come unto me, and forbid them not:
for of such is the kingdom of God."
~~~ Mark 10:13-14

"Hear thou, my son, and be wise,
and guide thine heart in the way."
~~~ Proverbs 23:19

"The LORD shall increase you more and more, you and your children.
Ye are blessed of the LORD which made heaven and earth."
~~~ Psalm 115:14-15

"Lo, children are an heritage of the LORD:
and the fruit of the womb is his reward."
~~~ Psalm 127:3

~~~~~~~~~~~

These passages are but a glimpse into the Word of God on this subject.
You are encouraged to read the Holy Bible every day,
and walk in the light of His truth for godly living.

Passages On
Parenting

~ ~ ~ ~ ~

"Train up a child in the way he should go:
and when he is old, he will not depart from it."
~~~ Proverbs 22:6

"And, ye fathers, provoke not your children to wrath:
but bring them up in the nurture and admonition of the Lord."
~~~ Ephesians 6:4

"The LORD shall increase you more and more, you and your children.
Ye are blessed of the LORD which made heaven and earth."
~~~ Psalm 115:14-15

"Lo, children are an heritage of the LORD:
and the fruit of the womb is his reward."
~~~ Psalm 127:3

"Fathers, provoke not your children to anger,
lest they be discouraged."
~~~ Colossians 3:21

"Chasten thy son while there is hope,
and let not thy soul spare for his crying."
~~~ Proverbs 19:18

"The father of the righteous shall greatly rejoice: and he that
begetteth a wise child shall have joy of him."
~~~ Proverbs 23:24

"Correct thy son, and he shall give thee rest;
yea, he shall give delight unto thy soul."
~~~ Proverbs 29:17

~~~~~~~~~~

*These passages are but a glimpse into the Word of God on this subject.
You are encouraged to read the Holy Bible every day,
and walk in the light of His truth for godly living.*

Passages On
Growing Old

~ ~ ~ ~ ~

"With the ancient is wisdom; and in length of days understanding."
~~~ Job 12:12

"But speak thou the things which become sound doctrine:
That the aged men be sober, grave, temperate,
sound in faith, in charity, in patience.
The aged women likewise, that they be in behaviour as becometh
holiness, not false accusers, not given to much wine,
teachers of good things;
That they may teach the young women to be sober,
to love their husbands, to love their children,
To be discreet, chaste, keepers at home, good, obedient to their
own husbands, that the word of God be not blasphemed."
~~~ Titus 2:1-5

"The hoary head is a crown of glory,
if it be found in the way of righteousness."
~~~ Proverbs 16:31

"Children's children are the crown of old men;
and the glory of children are their fathers."
~~~ Proverbs 17:6

"The righteous shall flourish like the palm tree:
he shall grow like a cedar in Lebanon.
Those that be planted in the house of the LORD
shall flourish in the courts of our God."
~~~ Psalm 92:12-13

"Now also when I am old and greyheaded,
O God, forsake me not;
until I have shewed thy strength unto this generation,
and thy power to every one that is to come."
~~~ Psalm 71:18

~~~~~~~~~~

These passages are but a glimpse into the Word of God on this subject.
You are encouraged to read the Holy Bible every day,
and walk in the light of His truth for godly living.

Passages On
Anger

~ ~ ~ ~ ~

"Be not hasty in thy spirit to be angry:
for anger resteth in the bosom of fools."
~~~ Ecclesiastes 7:9

"Cease from anger, and forsake wrath:
fret not thyself in any wise to do evil."
~~~ Psalm 37:8

"Wherefore, my beloved brethren, let every man be swift to hear,
slow to speak, slow to wrath:
For the wrath of man worketh not the righteousness of God."
~~~ James 1:19-20

"Be ye angry, and sin not: let not the sun go down upon your wrath:
Neither give place to the devil."
~~~ Ephesians 4:26-27

"I will therefore that men pray every where,
lifting up holy hands, without wrath and doubting."
~~~ 1 Timothy 2:8

"Stand in awe, and sin not:
commune with your own heart upon your bed, and be still."
~~~ Psalm 4:4

"He that is soon angry dealeth foolishly:
and a man of wicked devices is hated."
~~~ Proverbs 14:17

"A wrathful man stirreth up strife:
but he that is slow to anger appeaseth strife."
~~~ Proverbs 15:18

"A violent man enticeth his neighbour,
and leadeth him into the way that is not good."
~~~ Proverbs 16:29

"Make no friendship with an angry man;
and with a furious man thou shalt not go:
Lest thou learn his ways, and get a snare to thy soul."
~~~ Proverbs 22:24-25

"Scornful men bring a city into a snare:
but wise men turn away wrath."
~~~ Proverbs 29:8

~~~~~~~~~~

*These passages are but a glimpse into the Word of God on this subject.
You are encouraged to read the Holy Bible every day,
and walk in the light of His truth for godly living.*

Passages On
Loneliness

~ ~ ~ ~ ~

"Draw nigh to God, and he will draw nigh to you."
~~~ James 4:8

"As the mountains are round about Jerusalem,
so the Lord is round about his people
from henceforth even for ever."
~~~ Psalm 125:2

"The Lord is nigh unto all them that call upon him,
to all that call upon him in truth."
~~~ Psalm 145:18

"For none of us liveth to himself, and no man dieth to himself."
~~~ Romans 14:7

"Let your conversation be without covetousness;
and be content with such things as ye have:
for he hath said, I will never leave thee, nor forsake thee."
~~~ Hebrews 13:5

"Let not your heart be troubled:
ye believe in God, believe also in me.
In my Father's house are many mansions:
if it were not so, I would have told you.
I go to prepare a place for you.
And if I go and prepare a place for you,
I will come again, and receive you unto myself;
that where I am, there ye may be also."
~~~ John 14:1-3

"If ye love me, keep my commandments.
And I will pray the Father, and he shall give you another Comforter,
that he may abide with you for ever;
Even the Spirit of truth; whom the world cannot receive,
because it seeth him not, neither knoweth him:
but ye know him; for he dwelleth with you, and shall be in you."
~~~ John 14:15-17

"Jesus answered and said unto him, If a man love me,
he will keep my words: and my Father will love him, and we will
come unto him, and make our abode with him."
~~~ John 14:23

"God setteth the solitary in families:
he bringeth out those which are bound with chains:
but the rebellious dwell in a dry land."
~~~ Psalm 68:6

"Teaching them to observe all things whatsoever I have
commanded you: and, lo, I am with you always,
even unto the end of the world. Amen."
~~~ Matthew 18:20

~~~~~~~~~~

*These passages are but a glimpse into the Word of God on this subject.
You are encouraged to read the Holy Bible every day,
and walk in the light of His truth for godly living.*

Passages On
Sleep & Peace

~ ~ ~ ~ ~

"I will both lay me down in peace, and sleep:
for thou, LORD, only makest me dwell in safety."
~~~ Psalm 4:8

"Be anxious for nothing,
but in everything by prayer and supplication with thanksgiving
let your requests be made known to God.
And the peace of God, which surpasses all comprehension,
will guard your hearts and your minds in Christ Jesus."
~~~ Philippians 4:6-7, NASB

"I will bless the LORD, who hath given me counsel:
my reins also instruct me in the night seasons."
~~~ Psalm 16:7

"The LORD will give strength unto his people;
the LORD will bless his people with peace."
~~~ Psalm 29:11

"Great peace have they which love thy law:
and nothing shall offend them."
~~~ Psalm 119:165

"It is vain for you to rise up early, to sit up late,
to eat the bread of sorrows: for so he giveth his beloved sleep."
~~~ Psalm 127:2

"Peace I leave with you, my peace I give unto you:
not as the world giveth, give I unto you.
Let not your heart be troubled, neither let it be afraid."
~~~ John 14:27

"These things I have spoken unto you, that in me ye might have
peace. In the world ye shall have tribulation:
but be of good cheer; I have overcome the world."
~~~ John 16:33

"O that thou hadst hearkened to my commandments!
then had thy peace been as a river,
and thy righteousness as the waves of the sea."
~~~ Isaiah 48:18

"Glory to God in the highest,
and on earth peace, good will toward men."
~~~ Luke 2:14

"And let the peace of God rule in your hearts,
to the which also ye are called in one body; and be ye thankful."
~~~ Colossians 3:15

"Now the Lord of peace himself give you peace always by all means.
The Lord be with you all."
~~~ 2 Thessalonians 3:16

~~~~~~~~~~

*These passages are but a glimpse into the Word of God on this subject.
You are encouraged to read the Holy Bible every day,
and walk in the light of His truth for godly living.*

Passages On
Gossip

~ ~ ~ ~ ~

"A talebearer revealeth secrets:
but he that is of a faithful spirit concealeth the matter."
~~~ Proverbs 11:13

"A wicked doer giveth heed to false lips;
and a liar giveth ear to a naughty tongue."
~~~ Proverbs 17:4

"The words of a talebearer are as wounds,
and they go down into the innermost parts of the belly."
~~~ Proverbs 18:8

"An ungodly witness scorneth judgment:
and the mouth of the wicked devoureth iniquity."
~~~ Proverbs 19:28

"He that goeth about as a talebearer revealeth secrets:
therefore meddle not with him that flattereth with his lips."
~~~ Proverbs 20:19

"Where no wood is, there the fire goeth out:
so where there is no talebearer, the strife ceaseth."
~~~ Proverbs 26:20

"Thou shalt not raise a false report:
put not thine hand with the wicked to be an unrighteous witness."
~~~ Exodus 23:1

"Well reported of for good works; if she have brought up children,
if she have lodged strangers, if she have washed the saints' feet,
if she have relieved the afflicted,
if she have diligently followed every good work.
But the younger widows refuse: for when they have begun
to wax wanton against Christ, they will marry;
Having damnation, because they have cast off their first faith.
And withal they learn to be idle, wandering about from
house to house; and not only idle, but tattlers also and busybodies,
speaking things which they ought not.
I will therefore that the younger women marry,
bear children, guide the house, give none occasion
to the adversary to speak reproachfully.
For some are already turned aside after Satan."
~~~ 1 Timothy 5:10-15

"But I say unto you, That every idle word that men shall speak,
they shall give account thereof in the day of judgment.
For by thy words thou shalt be justified,
and by thy words thou shalt be condemned."
~~~ Matthew 12:36-37

~~~~~~~~~~

These passages are but a glimpse into the Word of God on this subject.
You are encouraged to read the Holy Bible every day,
and walk in the light of His truth for godly living.

Passages On
Money & Wealth

~ ~ ~ ~ ~

"But godliness with contentment is great gain.
For we brought nothing into this world,
and it is certain we can carry nothing out.
And having food and raiment let us be therewith content.
But they that will be rich fall into temptation and a snare,
and into many foolish and hurtful lusts,
which drown men in destruction and perdition.
For the love of money is the root of all evil:
which while some coveted after, they have erred from the faith,
and pierced themselves through with many sorrows."
~~~ 1 Timothy 6:6-10

"He that loveth silver shall not be satisfied with silver;
nor he that loveth abundance with increase: this is also vanity."
~~~ Ecclesiastes 5:10

"There is that scattereth, and yet increaseth; and there is that
withholdeth more than is meet, but it tendeth to poverty.
The liberal soul shall be made fat:
and he that watereth shall be watered also himself."
~~~ Proverbs 11:24-25

"Honour the LORD with thy substance,
and with the firstfruits of all thine increase:
So shall thy barns be filled with plenty,
and thy presses shall burst out with new wine."
~~~ Proverbs 3:9-10

"Distributing to the necessity of saints;
given to hospitality."
~~~ Romans 12:13

"Every man according as he purposeth in his heart,
so let him give; not grudgingly, or of necessity:
for God loveth a cheerful giver."
~~~ 2 Corinthians 9:7

"I have shewed you all things, how that so labouring ye ought to
support the weak, and to remember the words of the Lord Jesus,
how he said, It is more blessed to give than to receive."
~~~ Acts 20:35

~~~~~~~~~~

*These passages are but a glimpse into the Word of God on this subject.
You are encouraged to read the Holy Bible every day,
and walk in the light of His truth for godly living.*

Passages On
Work

~ ~ ~ ~ ~

"In all labour there is profit:
but the talk of the lips tendeth only to penury."
~~~ Proverbs 14:23

"Whether therefore ye eat, or drink, or whatsoever ye do,
do all to the glory of God."
~~~ Psalm 37:23

"And whatsoever ye do, do it heartily, as to the Lord,
and not unto men;
Knowing that of the Lord ye shall receive the reward
of the inheritance: for ye serve the Lord Christ."
~~~ Colossians 3:23-24

"But let every man prove his own work, and then shall he have
rejoicing in himself alone, and not in another.
For every man shall bear his own burden."
~~~ Galatians 6:4-5

"Labour not for the meat which perisheth, but for that meat which
endureth unto everlasting life, which the Son of man shall give unto
you: for him hath God the Father sealed."
~~~ John 6:27

"I must work the works of him that sent me, while it is day:
the night cometh, when no man can work."
~~~ John 9:4

"And there are diversities of operations,
but it is the same God which worketh all in all."
~~~ 1 Corinthians 12:6

"He that tilleth his land shall be satisfied with bread:
but he that followeth vain persons is void of understanding."
~~~ Proverbs 12:11

"He also that is slothful in his work
is brother to him that is a great waster."
~~~ Proverbs 18:9

"Labour not to be rich: cease from thine own wisdom."
~~~ Proverbs 23:4

~~~~~~~~~~~

*These passages are but a glimpse into the Word of God on this subject.
You are encouraged to read the Holy Bible every day,
and walk in the light of His truth for godly living.*

Passages On
Poverty

~ ~ ~ ~ ~

"Therefore I say unto you, Take no thought for your life, what ye shall eat, or what ye shall drink; nor yet for your body, what ye shall put on. Is not the life more than meat, and the body than raiment?"
~~~ Matthew 6:25

"Better is little with the fear of the LORD
than great treasure and trouble therewith."
~~~ Proverbs 15:16

"Better is the poor that walketh in his uprightness,
than he that is perverse in his ways, though he be rich."
~~~ Proverbs 28:6

"For thou hast been a strength to the poor, a strength to the needy in his distress, a refuge from the storm, a shadow from the heat, when the blast of the terrible ones is as a storm against the wall."
~~~ Isaiah 25:4

"The righteous considereth the cause of the poor:
but the wicked regardeth not to know it."
~~~ Proverbs 29:7

"I know that the LORD will maintain the cause of the afflicted,
and the right of the poor."
~~~ Psalm 140:12

"Remove far from me vanity and lies: give me neither poverty
nor riches; feed me with food convenient for me:
Lest I be full, and deny thee, and say, Who is the LORD?
or lest I be poor, and steal, and take the name of my God in vain."
~~~ Proverbs 30:8-9

"Open thy mouth for the dumb
in the cause of all such as are appointed to destruction.
Open thy mouth, judge righteously,
and plead the cause of the poor and needy."
~~~ Proverbs 31:8-9

"The LORD is my shepherd; I shall not want."
~~~ Psalm 23:1

~~~~~~~~~~

*These passages are but a glimpse into the Word of God on this subject.
You are encouraged to read the Holy Bible every day,
and walk in the light of His truth for godly living.*

Passages On
Laziness

~ ~ ~ ~ ~

"That ye be not slothful, but followers of them who through faith
and patience inherit the promises."
~~~ Hebrews 6:12

"How long wilt thou sleep, O sluggard?
when wilt thou arise out of thy sleep?
Yet a little sleep, a little slumber,
a little folding of the hands to sleep:
So shall thy poverty come as one that travelleth,
and thy want as an armed man."
~~~ Proverbs 6:9-11

"Slothfulness casteth into a deep sleep;
and an idle soul shall suffer hunger."
~~~ Proverbs 19:15

"For even when we were with you, this we commanded you,
that if any would not work, neither should he eat."
~~~ 2 Thessalonians 3:10

"He becometh poor that dealeth with a slack hand:
but the hand of the diligent maketh rich."
~~~ Proverbs 10:4

"Now we command you, brethren, in the name of our Lord Jesus
Christ, that ye withdraw yourselves from every brother that walketh
disorderly, and not after the tradition which he received of us."
~~~ 2 Thessalonians 3:6

~~~~~~~~~~

*These passages are but a glimpse into the Word of God on this subject.
You are encouraged to read the Holy Bible every day,
and walk in the light of His truth for godly living.*

Passages On
Grief & Sorrow

~ ~ ~ ~ ~

"For godly sorrow worketh repentance to salvation not to be
repented of: but the sorrow of the world worketh death."
~~~ 2 Corinthians 7:10

"The LORD is nigh unto them that are of a broken heart; and saveth
such as be of a contrite spirit."
~~~ Psalm 34:18

"Why art thou cast down, O my soul? and why art thou disquieted
within me? hope in God: for I shall yet praise him,
who is the health of my countenance, and my God."
~~~ Psalm 43:5

"My soul melteth for heaviness:
strengthen thou me according unto thy word."
~~~ Psalm 119:28

"He healeth the broken in heart, and bindeth up their wounds."
~~~ Psalm 147:3

"Rejoice with them that do rejoice,
and weep with them that weep."
~~~ Romans 12:15

"Blessed are ye that weep now: for ye shall laugh."
~~~ Luke 6:21

"Jesus wept."
~~~ John 11:35

"Then saith He unto them, My soul is exceeding sorrowful, even unto death: tarry ye here, and watch with me."
~~~ Matthew 26:38

"And the ransomed of the LORD shall return, and come to Zion with songs and everlasting joy upon their heads: they shall obtain joy and gladness, and sorrow and sighing shall flee away."
~~~ Isaiah 35:10

"Surely he hath borne our griefs, and carried our sorrows: yet we did esteem him stricken, smitten of God, and afflicted."
~~~ Isaiah 53:4

"He will swallow up death in victory; and the Lord GOD will wipe away tears from off all faces; and the rebuke of his people shall he take away from off all the earth: for the LORD hath spoken it."
~~~ Isaiah 25:8

~~~~~~~~~~

These passages are but a glimpse into the Word of God on this subject. You are encouraged to read the Holy Bible every day, and walk in the light of His truth for godly living.

Passages On
Spiritual Gifts

~ ~ ~ ~ ~

"For I would that all men were even as I myself.
But every man hath his proper gift of God,
one after this manner, and another after that."
~~~ 1 Corinthians 7:7

"Now there are diversities of gifts, but the same Spirit."
~~~ 1 Corinthians 12:4

"But the manifestation of the Spirit
is given to every man to profit withal.
For to one is given by the Spirit the word of wisdom;
to another the word of knowledge by the same Spirit;
To another faith by the same Spirit;
to another the gifts of healing by the same Spirit;
To another the working of miracles; to another prophecy;
to another discerning of spirits; to another divers kinds of tongues;
to another the interpretation of tongues:
But all these worketh that one and the selfsame Spirit,
dividing to every man severally as he will."
~~~ 1 Corinthians 12:7-11

"So we, being many, are one body in Christ,
and every one members one of another.
Having then gifts differing according to the grace
that is given to us, whether prophecy,
let us prophesy according to the proportion of faith;
Or ministry, let us wait on our ministering:
or he that teacheth, on teaching;
Or he that exhorteth, on exhortation: he that giveth,
let him do it with simplicity; he that ruleth, with diligence;

he that sheweth mercy, with cheerfulness.
Let love be without dissimulation. Abhor that which is evil;
cleave to that which is good."
~~~ Romans 12:5-9

"And he gave some, apostles; and some, prophets;
and some, evangelists; and some, pastors and teachers;
For the perfecting of the saints, for the work of the ministry,
for the edifying of the body of Christ:
Till we all come in the unity of the faith,
and of the knowledge of the Son of God, unto a perfect man,
unto the measure of the stature of the fullness of Christ:
That we henceforth be no more children, tossed to and fro, and
carried about with every wind of doctrine, by the sleight of men,
and cunning craftiness, whereby they lie in wait to deceive;
But speaking the truth in love, may grow up into him in all things,
which is the head, even Christ:
From whom the whole body fitly joined together and compacted by
that which every joint supplieth, according to the effectual
working in the measure of every part,
maketh increase of the body unto the edifying of itself in love."
~~~ Ephesians 4:11-16

"As every man hath received the gift,
even so minister the same one to another,
as good stewards of the manifold grace of God."
~~~ 1 Peter 4:10

~~~~~~~~~~

These passages are but a glimpse into the Word of God on this subject.
You are encouraged to read the Holy Bible every day,
and walk in the light of His truth for godly living.

Passages On
Help

~ ~ ~ ~ ~

"Fear thou not; for I am with thee: be not dismayed; for I am thy
God: I will strengthen thee; yea, I will help thee; yea,
I will uphold thee with the right hand of my righteousness.
Behold, all they that were incensed against thee shall be ashamed
and confounded: they shall be as nothing;
and they that strive with thee shall perish.
Thou shalt seek them, and shalt not find them, even them that
contended with thee: they that war against thee shall be as
nothing, and as a thing of nought.
For I the LORD thy God will hold thy right hand,
saying unto thee, Fear not; I will help thee."
~~~ Isaiah 41:10-13

"I will lift up mine eyes unto the hills,
from whence cometh my help.
My help cometh from the LORD,
which made heaven and earth."
~~~ Psalm 121:1-2

"The Lord knoweth how to deliver the godly out of temptations,
and to reserve the unjust unto the day of judgment to be punished:
But chiefly them that walk after the flesh in the lust of uncleanness,
and despise government. Presumptuous are they,
selfwilled, they are not afraid to speak evil of dignities."
~~~ 2 Peter 2:9-10

"But my God shall supply all your need
According to his riches in glory by Christ Jesus."
~~~ Philippians 4:19

"Trust in the LORD with all thine heart;
and lean not unto thine own understanding.
In all thy ways acknowledge him, and he shall direct thy paths."
~~~ Proverbs 3:5-6

"And all things, whatsoever ye shall ask in prayer,
believing, ye shall receive."
~~~Matthew 21:22

"Help me, O LORD my God: O save me according to thy mercy:
That they may know that this is thy hand;
that thou, LORD, hast done it."
~~~ Psalm 109:26-27

"Therefore I say unto you, Take no thought for your life,
what ye shall eat, or what ye shall drink; nor yet for your body,
what ye shall put on. Is not the life more than meat,
and the body than raiment?
Behold the fowls of the air: for they sow not,
neither do they reap, nor gather into barns; yet your heavenly
Father feedeth them. Are ye not much better than they?
Which of you by taking thought can add one cubit unto his stature?
And why take ye thought for raiment? Consider the lilies of the
field, how they grow; they toil not, neither do they spin:
And yet I say unto you, That even Solomon in all his glory
was not arrayed like one of these.
Wherefore, if God so clothe the grass of the field,
which to day is, and to morrow is cast into the oven,
shall he not much more clothe you, O ye of little faith?
Therefore take no thought, saying, What shall we eat? or,
What shall we drink? or, Wherewithal shall we be clothed?
(For after all these things do the Gentiles seek:) for your heavenly
Father knoweth that ye have need of all these things.
But seek ye first the kingdom of God, and his righteousness;
and all these things shall be added unto you."
~~~ Matthew 6:25-33

"The LORD preserveth the simple:
I was brought low, and he helped me."
~~~ Psalm 116:6

"Be anxious for nothing,
but in everything by prayer and supplication with thanksgiving
let your requests be made known to God.
And the peace of God, which surpasses all comprehension,
will guard your hearts and your minds in Christ Jesus."
~~~ Philippians 4:6-7, NASB

~~~~~~~~~~

*These passages are but a glimpse into the Word of God on this subject.
You are encouraged to read the Holy Bible every day,
and walk in the light of His truth for godly living.*

About the Author
Judge Hal Moroz

~ ~ ~ ~ ~

"A wise man will hear, and will increase learning;
and a man of understanding shall attain unto wise counsels:
To understand a proverb, and the interpretation;
the words of the wise, and their dark sayings."
~~~ Proverbs 1:5-6

"Hear counsel, and receive instruction,
that thou mayest be wise in thy latter end."
~~~ Proverbs 19:20

"And the things that thou hast heard of me among many witnesses,
the same commit thou to faithful men,
who shall be able to teach others also."
~~~ 2 Timothy 2:2

~ ~ ~ ~ ~

Hal Moroz is an attorney & counselor at law, as well as a former Judge. He served as both a county Judge and a city Chief Judge. Hal is also a retired U.S. Army officer, having served in the Airborne Infantry. His journey through life includes experience as a law professor, educator, public speaker, university vice president, candidate for the United States Congress, and **entrepreneur**.

Judge Moroz identifies his greatest blessings as having the saving grace of Christ Jesus in his life, a good and godly wife, Denise, of more than three decades, and two wonderful children, William and Heather.

Hal and his wife, Denise, a Registered Nurse, reside in the great State of Georgia. Their primary goal is to grow in their personal relationship with the Lord, and, as the apostle Paul states in Romans 8:29, *"to be conformed to the image of His Son."* They are active in the Law, Healthcare, Politics, and Ministry, and attend the First Baptist Church of Atlanta.

~ ~ ~ ~ ~

Hal Moroz can be reached through an internet search
or through his email at: hal@morozlaw.com or his website:
MorozLaw.com

~~~~~~~~~

*"Whether therefore ye eat, or drink, or whatsoever ye do,
do all to the glory of God."*
~~~ Psalm 37:23

Postscript
Acknowledgements

~ ~ ~ ~ ~

"In every thing give thanks:
for this is the will of God in Christ Jesus concerning you."
~~~ 1 Thessalonians 5:18

~ ~ ~ ~ ~

I am thankful for all things! And, in particular, I would like to extend my thanks and acknowledge the support and encouragement of many friends, and I do mean friends, without whom this work would not have been possible.

My wife, Denise Moroz
My son, William Moroz
My daughter, Heather Moroz
Dr. Charles F. Stanley, First Baptist Church, Atlanta
Paul & Vickie Hafer, **The Lighthouse WECC 89.3 FM** Christian Radio
Pastor Rick Taylor
Pastor Jimmy Haines
Pastor John Pennington
Judge Kathe Loeffler
Hal Watkins
Dr. Jerry Falwell, *now with the Lord*
And, above all

Our Lord & Saviour Jesus Christ ...

"For God so loved the world, that He gave His only begotten Son,
for whosoever believeth in Him should not perish,
but have everlasting life."
~~~ John 3:16